ILLUSTRATIONS

OF

INDIAN ORNITHOLOGY

ILLUSTRATIONS

OF

INDIAN ORNITHOLOGY

BY T. C. JERDON, ESQ.

GYAN

Published by

Gyan Publishing House
5, Ansari Road
Daryaganj, New Delhi-110002
Phone: 011-47034999, 9811692060
E-mail: books@gyanbooks.com

Distribution Network
gyanbooks.com
India, USA, Canada, UK, Australia

ISBN: 978-81-212-5989-7 (PB)
First Published, 1847

2nd Impression 2024

Printed at: Gyan Press, Delhi.

ILLUSTRATIONS OF INDIAN ORNITHOLOGY
Author: T. C. JERDON

ILLUSTRATIONS

OF

INDIAN ORNITHOLOGY,

CONTAINING

FIFTY FIGURES

OF

NEW, UNFIGURED AND INTERESTING SPECIES OF BIRDS,

CHIEFLY FROM THE SOUTH OF INDIA.

BY T. C. JERDON, ESQ.

MADRAS MEDICAL ESTABLISHMENT.

MADRAS:

PRINTED BY P. R. HUNT, AMERICAN MISSION PRESS.

1847.

INTRODUCTION.

It is with much satisfaction that the Author has brought this work to a conclusion, though so long delayed by various obstacles. Forty-seven distinct species of Birds are represented in the fifty plates. The great majority of them are figured here for the first time, and either improved figures, or different states of plumage, compose the remainder of the drawings. Three of the birds are from the Himalayas, and one from Ceylon—all the rest inhabit the peninsula of India.

CONTENTS.

INTRODUCTORY NOTICE.

The first part of the ILLUSTRATIONS OF INDIAN ORNITHOLOGY is at length presented to the Public, after a greater delay in the publication than the Author was led to expect.

The ground-work and branches are from the pencil of a highly talented amateur Artist, and the Author here begs leave to tender his most grateful acknowledgments for his very valuable aid, which has contributed not a little to set off the drawings and embellish the work. Several of the plates, however, viz. Nos., 1, 2, 3, 4, 5, 6 and 12 were printed off before the Author became acquainted with that gentleman. Thirty additional copies of these plates being afterwards found necessary to meet the increasing list of Subscribers, the same Officer added a ground-work to these. The colourists were instructed to paint in to those first printed similar to that of the additional lithographs; but, as might have been expected, they have not executed this part so well as the Author could have wished, and they were not allowed to finish all the copies. In consequence of this a difference, more marked in some than others, will be found among the plates mentioned above; and I trust that this explanation may prove sufficient to those who have the opportunity of comparing the two sets.

The 2d No. being entirely printed and partially coloured, will appear at no very distant interval, and the nature of its contents will probably make it more attractive than the present number.

Should the publication of the present series of fifty birds be, as there is every reason to anticipate, successful enough to repay the Author for the heavy expenses he has incurred, it will, immediately on completion, be followed by a second set of fifty more birds, and the two series will then include a very considerable number of the unfigured species of Peninsular India.

A classified Index will be given with the concluding No. which will notice any corrections of nomenclature that may be required.

NELLORE : *November 3d,* 1843.

I

Nisaetus strenuus,

Printed by C. V. Kistnarajoo,

ORD. RAPTORES.

TRIBE—FALCONIDÆ.

FAM. AQUILINÆ.

GENUS NISÆTUS—Hodgson.

PLATE I.

NISÆTUS GRANDIS—Hodgson.

YOUNG FEMALE.

LARGE HAWK-EAGLE.

Synon.—*Nisætus niveus,* Jerdon—Madras Journal of Literature and Science, No. 24.

Mhorunghee, in Hindustani—*Salwa,* in Teloogoo—*Rajalee,* in Tamool.

THE group of rapacious birds to which this fine Eagle belongs, was first separated by Mr. Hodgson, in a paper published in the 6th volume of the Journal of the Asiatic Society of Bengal, and the genus is there characterized as follows:—"Bill short, at base as high as broad, distinguished by compression without feebleness, strongly festooned, nares large, vertical, elliptic, angulated and wholly lateral in exposure—wings short, firm, fifth quill longest—tail long, firm and square—tarsi elevate, but not feeble, wholly feathered—digits elongated, nervous, the inner fore and the hind highly developed—acropodia reticulate with three or four scales next each talon—talons immense, very unequal, strong and acute—head usually crested."—Mr. Blyth, the zealous and able Curator of the Museum of the Asiatic Society at Calcutta seems to think that this genus is not separable from *Spizætus* of authors. Not having had an opportunity of examining any of the African and South American Eagles classed in that genus, I cannot attempt to decide the point, but I think it likely there will be found some shades of difference, warranting at all events a sub-generic distinction. This I consider to be the more likely as the genus is not one of universal occurrence. Moreover, Swainson has separated the *Falco cristatellus,* an undoubted member of this group, from the African crested Eagles, retaining however *Spizætus* for the Indian Bird, and classing the others under the genus *Harpyia.* Sir W. Jardine too in a letter to me writing of the present subject says 'modified characters will receive both this, and *cristatellus.*' I therefore prefer for the present retaining Hodgson's excellent name as being more appropriate to the habits as well as structure of the birds of this group than the name *Spizætus.*—Mr. G. R. Gray, in his Genera of Birds has put *Nisætus* as a synonym of *Limnætus.* This is of course a grievous error, this latter genus being described as having all the claws nearly *equal* and *small.*

The present species or large Hawk-Eagle was first described and named by Mr. Hodgson in the 5th volume of the Journal of the Asiatic Society. When I drew up the Catalogue of Peninsular Birds in the Madras Journal, I was unaware of Hodgson's paper, and referred this bird to the *Falco niveus* of authors, with the meagre descriptions of which in the books of reference I had access to, it indeed sufficiently agrees. I have however since ascertained it to be distinct.* I shall now give a description of the species represented here taken partly from my own observations, and partly from the obliging communications of Mr. Blyth.

Young bird.—Plumage above pale brown with the shaft and tip of each feather somewhat darker. Beneath, under wing-coverts and tibial plumes of a rusty white (in some deeply stained with ferruginous) with a very narrow mesial pale brown stripe on the feathers, almost obsolete in some.—Tail above closely and numerously barred with brown, on a pale brown ground.

Adult.—Above deep aquiline or wood brown. Beneath, pure white with a dark brown mesial line to each feather; broader in general in the female, and most developed on the belly, on which in old birds the brown hue predominates, and takes the form of bars. Under wing-coverts dark brown—under tail-coverts white banded brown—tibial plumes deep brown, freckled whitish—tail hoary grey with seven bars and a broad subterminal one.

An intermediate state of plumage is marked by the pale edging to the feathers

* The name *Strenuus,* was printed on the Plate before I was aware that the specimen from which the drawing was taken was identical in species with *grandis.*

of the back, by the less development of the mesial markings of the feathers of the lower plumage, and by the paler tint of the tibial and tarsal plumes.

At all ages the feathers of the nape are margined with whitish (or pale brown in some) and their bases are conspicuously white. Bill plumbeous, black at tip—cere and feet pale greenish yellow—irides bright gamboge yellow. Dimensions—Length of a male 26 to 27 inches—wing from flexure $17\frac{1}{2}$ to 18 inches—tail 11—bill straight to gape 2—tarsus $3\frac{1}{2}$—centre digit $2\frac{4}{10}$—do. claw $1\frac{2}{10}$. Length of female 29 to 30 inches—wing $20\frac{1}{4}$—tail $12\frac{1}{2}$ to 13.

The large Hawk-Eagle is dispersed over the whole continent of India from the Himalayas to Cape Comorin, but cannot be said to be an abundant species, though few districts are not occasionally frequented or visited by a pair of them. It chiefly affects the more wooded and jungly districts, and especially the neighbourhood of hills and mountain ranges. It is much on the wing, sailing at a great height; and making its appearance at certain spots in the district it frequents always about the same hour. It may often be seen seated on the summit of a lofty tree, or on some overhanging rock. I have observed it chiefly on the Neilgherries, along the range of western and northern ghauts; also though more sparingly in the bare Deccan and Carnatic. The individual from which the present drawing was taken was killed in Guindy park at Madras.

It preys by preference on various kinds of game—hares, jungle fowl, spur fowl and partridges, and even on pea fowl—also on ducks, herons and other water fowl, and according to the testimony of Shikarees it has been known to strike down the douk, (*Tantalus leucocephalus.*) Most native Falconers too have stories to relate of its having carried off a favorite hawk. On one occasion on the Neilgherries, I observed it stoop successively at a spur-fowl, hare, and pea-fowl, each time unsuccessfully however, owing to the thickness of the jungle. A pair were also wont to resort to a village at the hills and carry off fowls. Mr. Elliot too mentions "that he once saw a pair of them nearly surprise a peacock, pouncing on him on the ground." Great havoc was committed among several pigeon-houses on the Neilgherries by a pair of these Eagles, and indeed I heard that one or two were completely devastated by them. The manner in which they captured the pigeons was described to me by two or three eye witnesses to be as follows:—On the pigeons taking flight, one of the Eagles pounced down from a vast height on the flock, but directing its swoop rather under the pigeons, than directly at them. Its mate watching the moment when, alarmed by the first swoop the pigeons rise in confusion, pounces unerringly on one of them and carries it off. The other Eagle having risen again also makes another stoop which is generally fatal. One of these birds shot in the act was presented to me by a gentleman, who had been a great sufferer by them. I have not yet been fortunate enough to meet with the nest of this Hawk-Eagle, but it is said by native Shikarees to build on steep and inaccessible cliffs, and to breed in January or February.

The other known Indian species of this group are:—1st, *Nisætus niveus.*—2d, *N. pulcher,* Hodgson.—3rd, *N. Kieieriin*;—and 4th, *N. cristatellus.* A fifth species has been merely indicated by Hodgson as *N. pallidus.* I shall here give a brief description of these four species from copious information afforded me by Mr. Blyth.

1st.—Nisætus niveus—Subcrested Hawk-Eagle.

Syn.—*Falco niveus,* Tem.—*F. caligatus,* Raffles ?—*Nis. Nipalensis,* Hodgson.

Young.—Above brown, the feathers with broad pale edgings, usually has a slightly developed occipital crest, sometimes found possessed of a long drooping occipital egret-like crest of two long feathers—beneath white, nearly spotless—tibial plumes white, regularly crossed with pale fulvous bands—under tail-coverts white spotted with brown—tail brown with five dark bands and a subterminal one broader and more distinct,—the tipwhitish—head and nape usually light fulvous with dark mesial stripes, extending by age—quills barred with blackish.

Intermediate age—Above dark aquiline brown, with pale edgings, obsolete on the interscapulars—beneath white with a dark mesial stripe down the throat and 2 lateral ones less defined—breast with brownish black drops on each plume—rest of the plumage beneath nearly all dark brown—tibial feathers and under tail feathers barred with dark brown and white—tail brown with an ashy tinge and banded as in the young bird.

Adult—Plumage entirely dusky black, dashed with ashy on the back—the under surface of the primaries anterior to their emargination and the under surface of the tail alone albescent—caudal bands only visible beneath—cere dark livid—irides light grey brown in young—bright yellow in adult—feet pale wax yellow. Length of a male about 25 inches—expanse of wings 49—wing 15—tail 11—bill at gape $1\frac{1}{2}$—tarsus $3\frac{1}{2}$. Female from 26 to $29\frac{1}{2}$ inches—expanse 54—wing $15\frac{3}{4}$—tail 11—bill $1\frac{7}{8}$—tarsus 4.

This species has a larger known geographical distribution than any other of the genus having been found in Bengal, the Himalayas, and Java.

Nisætus grandis.

2nd.—Nisætus pulcher, Hodgson.

Above deep brown, blackish on the crown and occipital crest which is 4 inches long—feathers of the nape pale at base and edges—beneath white, tinged with fulvous—chin blackish—central line of throat and two lateral ones also blackish—breast with broad longitudinal streaks—belly and flanks banded and mottled brown and white—under tail coverts the same—tibial plumes distinctly banded—tarsal plumes less so—upper tail coverts and quills also banded—tail with 5 dark broad bars on a brownish grey ground. Length of male 29 inches—wing 18—tail 13. Female 32—wing 19—tail 14½.

3rd.—Nisætus Kienierii, Red-bodied Hawk-Eagle.

Syn.—*Astur Kienierii,* De Sparre—Guerin Mag. de Zoologie, 1835.—*Nis. albogularis,* Tickell—Jour. As. Society, 1842.

Above black with a shade of brown—an occipital crest 2½ inches long—throat, neck, and breast, pure white, the sides of the last only with black streaks—belly, flanks, under tail coverts, legs, under surface of wings deep rufous, streaked with black on flanks—tail brown, obscurely banded—wings and tail beneath albescent, with narrow bands—ear coverts white at base, the rest rufous, each feather streaked with black—irides dark—cere wax yellow. The specimen from which this description was taken was probably in its second or third year; the younger bird as shown by some unmoulted feathers had the brown of the upper plumage only moderately dark. An apparently more advanced stage is described by De Sparre as quoted above. Plumage above and occipital crest, fine black, with copper reflections, most apparent on the wings—secondaries and ridge of wing edged with clear rufous—throat white—cheeks mixed with white black and red—neck and breast white with longitudinal medial black spots, most numerous and largest on the breast and these mixed with rufous spots—belly, abdomen and sides rufous, marked with numerous and large black medial spots—under tail coverts and legs unspotted rufous—tail black above, albescent beneath with black band. Length 22 inches—wing 16—tail 10—bill 1⅝—tarsus 3.

A single specimen was procured by Lieutenant Tickell at Chyebassa in Central India. The specimen described by De Sparre was said to be from the Himalayas and is in the collection of Prince Essling.

Illustrations of Indian Ornithology;

4th.—NISÆTUS CRISTATELLUS, Elliot—Madras Journal of Literature and Science, No. 25.

Syn.—*Falco. cristatellus,* Tem.

Judging from analogy with other species of this genus what is apparently the young state of this bird is thus described by Jardine. Above and occipital crest amber brown with pale margins to each feather, forehead white, head and nape yellowish brown, mixed with amber brown. Tail above brown, with seven narrow black bars, and white tip. Beneath, feathers of tarsi, and ridge of the wings white.

Apparently the second plumage is thus described by Lesson.

Above brown tinted with rufous—head and neck rufous streaked with brown, beneath white streaked with bright rufous, deepening in the flanks, inferior coverts and legs. Tail brownish rayed with dark brown.

A still more advanced age (Mr. Elliot's specimen) has the plumage above and occipital crest, fine deep brown, the latter nearly black, quills banded with dark brown. Tail with five bands. Beneath white, each feather with a large blackish brown drop, which occupies nearly the whole feather, flanks and lower part of abdomen nearly all brown. Tarsal feathers of a fawn tinge, spotted with brown.

Cere and orbits dark livid or plumbeous. Length, of male 24 inches—wing 16—tail $11\frac{2}{10}$—bill to gape $1\frac{7}{10}$—tarsus 4.

The specimen described by Jardine was said to have been taken on the coast of England. M. Lesson's specimen was from Ceylon, and Mr. Elliot's was procured at the foot of the Eastern Ghauts inland from Nellore. I may add that the description of this latter specimen has been taken partly from Mr. Elliot's, and partly from a drawing which that gentleman had taken of his specimen.

In comparing the descriptions of this bird with those of *Nisætus niveus,* it is impossible I think to avoid the supposition that they are identical. They are about the same size and relative dimensions. The description of the young state of each is nearly identical, and the more advanced state as described by Mr. Blyth of *N. niveus* only differ from that of Mr. Elliot's specimen in such a degree as we should expect in a bird of one less moult. The cere of both is described as being livid. It is represented very short in Mr. Elliot's drawing thus further corresponding with *niveus,* and lastly the geographical distribution of *niveus* being comparatively so extensive, we have every reason to expect its occurrence in Southern India. I may here state that I observed a bird apparently of this species in high jungle at the foot of the Neilgherries. It was seated on the summit of a high tree and had its crest raised. I was unfortunately unable to procure it.

In a future part of this publication I hope to be able to give a figure of the adult plumage of *Nisætus grandis.*

Leucocirca albofrontata,

Printed by C. V. Hästmaraj oc,

ORD. INSESSORES.

TRIBE—DENTIROSTRES.

FAM. MUSCICAPIDÆ.

GEN. LEUCOCIRCA.

PLATE II.

LEUCOCIRCA ALBOFRONTATA.

WHITE-BROWED FANTAIL.

Synon.—*Rhipidura albofrontata,* Franklin—Proc. Zool. Soc. 1831, page 116.
Muchurrea, Hindustani.

In the excellent volume on *Flycatchers* by Swainson, in the Naturalist's Library, this genus was first proposed to be separated from *Rhipidura;* the chiof distinctions being the bill more lengthened, broader at the base, and less compressed towards the tip, the bristles not quite so long, and the legs and feet more developed. It appears restricted to the tropics of the old world, more especially to India and its Islands.

The subject of our present plate was first described by Major Franklin, in his useful Catalogue of Birds procured by him on the banks of the Ganges and the Vindhian range of mountains, which was published in the Proceedings of the Zoological Society for 1831. It was also included by Colonel Sykes in his Catalogue of the Birds of the Dukhun, published in the same work, and I gave a brief account of its habits in my Catalogue of Birds of the Peninsula of India, published in the Madras Journal of Literature and Science. It would accordingly appear to have a tolerably extensive distribution over the continent of India, though it has not been found in Bengal, its place there being taken by the *Rhipidura fuscoventris* of Franklin, which I have not yet observed in the Peninsula, though it is included in Colonel Sykes' list. Towards the South of the Peninsula, the *White-browed Fantail* is only found at all common in those districts abounding in wood, and it is of frequent occurrence all along the Western coast, though not found, that I am aware, in the depths of the forests, preferring chiefly avenues of large trees, gardens, and the more open portions of the jungle. In the bare Carnatic, it is only met with now and then in large topes or groves of trees, and extensive gardens, and still more sparingly in some of the patches of low jungle found in the more hilly portions of this district. Towards the more Northern part of the Peninsula however, as I had an opportunity of observing at Jaulnah, N. Lat. 20°, it is much more common and diffused, and may be seen in every clump of trees or garden.

In its habits it appears to be the most active and restless of the whole family, continually flitting about from branch to branch, snapping up an insect on the wing every now and then, and raising its outspread tail, and lowering its wings, whenever it reseats itself on a twig. It hardly ever flies beyond a few feet after an insect, and seldom returns to the same perch, traversing in succession most of the branches of the tree, and not resting during even the heat of the day. I have usually seen it solitary, occasionally two or three in company. I have several times seen it alight on the ground, and on one or two occasions observed it seated on the back of a cow, and pursuing insects from this unusual perch. Its chief food consists of mosquitoes and other small dipterous insects, whence its Hindustani name.

It has a pleasing little song, which it warbles forth every now and then, consisting of several notes following each other in a regularly descending scale. Colonel Sykes speaking togetherof this bird, and *L. fuscoventris*, says, " The male has a very sweet note. He spreads and raises his tail over his head in hopping from bough to bough." Its popular name in Teloogoo is *Dasharee pitta*, a name which refers to the conspicuous white forehead and eyebrows, *Dasharee* being the Teloogoo name for the white stripe, with which certain of the Hindoos adorn their foreheads. I was informed that its name in Malayalum is *Manatee*, or *Washerman*, given from the continual upraising of its tail, the washermen in this country raising their clothes high above their heads and beating them on a stone. I am ignorant of any facts as to its nidification. The species is figured here for the first time I believe. I shall add a brief description of it, and a synopsis of the other Indian species.

Description.—Plumage above and neck in front, dusky black, darkest on head and neck, and palest on the tail—forehead, eyebrows extending to the nape, plumage beneath, a few spots on the wing coverts, and the tips of the tail feathers (except the two centre ones) white—chin and throat white mottled with black—irides dark brown—bill and legs blackish—length about 7 inches or $7\frac{1}{4}$—extent of wings 10—wing from flexure $3\frac{3}{10}$—bill at gape $\frac{6}{10}$—at front about $\frac{4}{10}$—tarsus $\frac{7}{10}$—tail $3\frac{7}{10}$—weight $6\frac{1}{2}$ drachms.

The other ascertained Indian species of this group are as follows:—

1.—*L. fuscoventris*—*Rhipidura fuscoventris* of Franklin, Proc. Zool. Soc. 1831, and Sykes—mentioned above.

2.—*L. pectoralis*, Jerdon—New species. Description—head and cheeks black—rest of plumage above dusky black—band across the breast black white spotted, chin blackish—throat white—abdomen and under tail coverts whitish, tinged with fulvous—feathers of the tail light dusky, all, except the centre ones, tipped lighter—bill and legs blackish—irides dark brown—length $6\frac{3}{4}$ inches—wing 3—tail $3\frac{8}{10}$—tarsus $\frac{7}{10}$—bill at front $\frac{7}{20}$—at gape $\frac{6}{10}$—weight $6\frac{1}{2}$ drachms.

In my Catalogue of Birds previously referred to, I mention under the head of *L. fuscoventris*, that I had observed that species on the Neilgherries, though I had not procured it. Since that time I obtained this bird and found it to be distinct and apparently undescribed, so I have accordingly characterized it as above. It frequents chiefly the warmer valleys at the edges of woods, and occasionally hedges and thickets. Its habits are much the same as those of its congeners.

3.—*L. hypoxantha*, Blyth.

Description.—Above of the usual dusky colour—eyestreak, and entire under parts brilliant-yellow—tail conspicuously white shafted with white interior edges to the feathers for their terminal half—length $4\frac{1}{2}$ inches. Hab. Darjeeling.

III

Zanclostomus viridirostris.

Printed by Litho. C V Kistnarajoo

ORD. INSESSORES.

TRIBE—SCANSORES.

FAM. CUCULIDÆ.

GEN. ZANCLOSTOMUS—*Swainson.*

PLATE III.

ZANCLOSTOMUS VIRIDIROSTRIS—*Jerdon.*

GREEN-BILLED CUCKOO.

Synon.—*Phænicophæus Jerdoni,* Blyth.—J. A. S. 1842—page 1095—not *Ph. viridirostris,* Eyton—P. Z. S. 1839.

I described this bird as apparently new in my Catalogue of Birds of the Indian Peninsula already referred to, and Mr. Blyth to whom I sent specimens so far assents to this that he has given it a new name, but he says, " In most particulars this bird agrees with Dr. Latham's description of his *Madagascar Cuckoo* the *Serisomus cristatus* of Swainson, or *Coucou Huppé de Madagascar* of Buffon, which Levaillant states is also found in some parts of India, Dr. Latham adding, that 'I find a similar one among the drawings of Mr. Daniell, found in Ceylon, and there called *Handee Kootah.*' No doubt the present species is alluded to in both cases." That the species found in Ceylon and figured by Daniell may be identical with our bird, I have very little doubt, but that the *Madagascar Cuckoo,* referred by Swainson to his genus *Serisomus* (which indeed appears to have been created purposely for it) be the same as the species here figured, no one, who compares the structure of the bill of the *Green-billed Cuckoo* with that of *Serisomus cristatus* (as given by Swainson in his Synopsis, evidently from nature) can for a moment imagine; and I presume that Mr. Blyth has drawn this hasty conclusion without referring to the figure here alluded to. Mr. Blyth moreover has included this bird in the genus *Phænicophæus* of Vieillot, though he says of it, and a nearly allied species, *Melias tristis* of Lesson, "the bill is still more compressed and proportionally smaller, assuming nearly the same form as in *Zanclostomus*, wherein Mr. Jerdon has even placed one of them." On referring to Swainson's definition of the two genera I am still inclined to place our present bird in the genus *Zanclostomus*, it may be as a somewhat aberrant species.

The *Green-billed Cuckoo* is dispersed over a great portion of the Peninsula of India, though by no means common except in some few localities. It has not as yet been procured in Bengal, but I have little doubt that it extends into Central India.

In the bare Carnatic and the Deccan it is chiefly to be met with in those districts where the land is much enclosed, as in part of the Zillah of Coimbatore, where large tracts of country are enclosed by thick and in many cases lofty hedges of various species of Euphorbia, which afford shelter and abundance of food to this bird. It is also to be found in patches of low and thorny jungle, more especially if, as is the case with many of the low ranges of hills in the Carnatic, bushes of Euphorbia form a prominent portion of the jungle. Throughout the West Coast where jungles and forests abound, it is much more common, especially in those parts where bamboos occur, and where numberless creepers entwine themselves and hang in luxuriant festoons from almost every tree. Such is the peculiarly appropriate haunt of our Cuckoo, which diligently searches the foliage for various species of mantis, grasshopper and locust, whose green colours and odd forms though assimilating so strongly to the plants on which they rest, are of but little avail against its keen and searching eye. It is usually found single, and when observed but seldom takes to flight, making its way most adroitly through the most tangled breakes or hedges, and concealing itself on the opposite side. I was informed that its Hindustani name is '*Kuppra Popeya*,' and in Teloogoo it is called by some *Wamanah Kakee*. I never heard its cry, and know nothing of its nidification.

Description.—General colour above dark greenish grey, the wings and tail glossy green, tail feathers tipped white ; beneath light dusky greyish, tinged with ferruginous on breast, and the feathers of the throat and neck dark at their bases. Length about 15 inches —of which the tail is nearly 10—wing $5\frac{1}{4}$—bill to forehead 1 inch—at gape $1\frac{1}{4}$—tarsus $1\frac{3}{10}$ths—weighs 2 oz. 12 drachms.

A closely allied species to this is the *Zanclostomus tristis*, *Melias tristis* of Lesson, and the *Phænicophæus longicandatus* of Blyth's Monograph of the Indian *Cuculidæ*, which that gentleman informs me he considers identical. This species inhabits Nepal and the

Tenasserim provinces. It bears a very close resemblance in colour to our Peninsular bird, but is much larger, being 23 inches long, of which the tail is 16¾. The only other ascertained Indian species of this genus is *Zanclostomus Sirkeer*, the *Eudynamys Sirkee* of Gray and Hardwick, and *Sirkee Cuckoo* of Latham, which I have found, though much more rarely, in the same localities as the last.

IV

Accipiter Besra,

Printed by E.V. Kistnarajoo,

ORD. RAPTORES.

TRIBE—FALCONIDÆ.

FAM. ACCIPITRINÆ.

GEN. ACCIPITER.

PLATE IV.

ACCIPITER BESRA—*Jerdon.*

THE BESRA HAWK.

Synon.—*Accip. minutus,* Auct. ?—Acc. *Dussumierii* of Sykes' Catalogue ?—Acc. *fringillarius,* Jerdon—Catalogue No. 35?—Acc. Besra do., No. 34, Madras Journal, No. XXIV. *Besra,* (the female.) *Dhotee,* (the male,) in Hindustani. *Vaishtapa Dyaga,* in Teloogoo. *Oor chitlee,* Canarese of the Halapyk caste.

At No. 34 of my Catalogue of Birds of Southern India, I very briefly indicated this species, from Mr. Elliot's notes, never having to my knowledge at that time seen the *Besra,* while under No. 35, I described a Hawk procured by me on the Coonoor pass of the Neilgherries in thick forest, which, if not identical with the *Besra,* is a very closely allied species. Since that Catalogue was published I have seen two living specimens of the *Besra,* and have procured the skin of another, and am thus enabled to present to the scientific world the accompanying figure and description, which latter, however, is much less complete, than I could have wished, as I am at present unable to give an account of the changes of plumage of this Hawk, so necessary to a full knowledge of the species. I trust however to be enabled to do so before this publication is finished. Although I suspect that the *Besra* may be the *Accipiter minutus* of authors, which though originally described from Malta, is said by Lesson to have been received from Ceylon and the Coromandel coast, yet as there is another small species of Sparrow Hawk (the *Khandesra*) also found here, I have placed it as a distinct species for the present, till specimens have been compared with those named *Acc. minutus* in European collections, unless the present figure and description be sufficient to guide Naturalists at Home in deciding the point. I think it very probable that the *Acc. Dussumierii* of Sykes' Catalogue be no other than this species, as it agrees in size, whilst his *Acc. Dukhunensis* is apparently the *F. Dussumierii* of Temminck.

The *Besra* is a comparatively rare Hawk, though well known, by name at least, to every native who takes an interest in hawking. Its permanent resorts are the large and lofty forests of Western India, and it is only after the breeding season is over, about July, that a few birds, usually young ones, straggle to various portions of the Eastern parts of the Peninsula, and there only to districts more than usually wooded or jungly. Here they remain a few months, and return again to the Western forests for the purpose of breeding. Mr. Elliot says that "he has only met with it in the Soonda jungles (in Canara) where it is taken young by a caste called *Halapyks*, and sold to falconers from Hyderabad." I have reason to believe that several individuals are annually captured on certain districts on the Eastern coast, where from time immemorial they have been known to resort to on migrating from the Western coast.

The *Besra* and other short winged Hawks, as well as occasionally the Luggur and some of the Falcons, are usually caught by what is called among Falconers the *Do Guz*. This is a small thin net from four to five feet long, and about three feet broad, stained of a dark colour, and fixed between two thin pieces of bamboo, by a cord on which it runs. The bamboos are fixed lightly in the ground, and a living bird is picketed about the middle of the net and not quite a foot distant from it. The Hawk makes a dash at the bird, which it sees struggling at its tether, and in the keenness of its rush, either not observing the net from its dark colour, or not heeding it, dashes into it, the two side sticks give way, and the net folds round the bird so effectually as to keep it almost from fluttering.

The *Besra* is said to be somewhat more difficult to train than most of the Hawks, and it is a delicate bird, and requires great care and attention, especially during the hot season. It is highly esteemed among Native Falconers, and sells for a considerable price. It is very speedy, and particularly active and clever in jungle, which its habits, as a denizen of the forests in its wild state, peculiarly fit it for. It is chiefly flown at the partridge, which it seizes in general with great ease and certainty; also occasionally at quails, snipes and doves. The male or *dhotee* is but seldom trained and is then flown at sparrows, brahminy mynas, *(pastor pagodarum)* and other small birds. I shall now give a description of this Hawk.

Male, 1st year.—Plumage above clear wood or hair brown, darkest on the head—

a few of the feathers at the bend of the wing faintly edged with rufous—ear coverts cinereous—throat white with a longitudinal dusky streak in the centre—plumage beneath white, with large brown marks, long, oval, and somewhat lanceolate on the breast, more rounded on the abdomen, and forming broad bars on the sides—tail with four dark brown bars on a pale ashy brown ground—leg feathers white, closely marked with small roundish brown marks—under tail-coverts pure white—bill blueish, black at tip—cere and orbitur skin pale greenish yellow—legs and feet pale yellowish green with a glaucous tinge—irides golden yellow, with an exterior circle of black—tarsus long, thin and compressed of apparently two long plates, one before and one behind. Length 10 inches—wing from flexure 6—tail 5—tarsus 2. The second quill is longer than other species of this genus—the third is equal to the fifth, and but slightly shorter than the fourth, which is longest. There are eight scutella on the posterior toe next the claw, seven on the internal, twenty-five on the centre, and seventeen on the external toe.

The specimen from which the accompanying figure was taken (as well two living birds I have seen) was beginning to moult, and the new feathers were of a dark cinereous or slaty hue, and Native Falconers assure me that such is the colour of the upper plumage of the *Besra* after its first moult and which it is said not again to change. If this be the case, the specimen I procured on the side of the Neilgherries formerly alluded to cannot well be this species, as it has tho upper plumage of dark clove brown, whilst the under feathers have the usual barred character of the Hawks after their first moult. It has the lower plumage white, numerously and broadly barred with rufous brown, mixed with dusky brown. The length of this bird was about 14 inches—wing $7\frac{1}{2}$—tail $5\frac{8}{10}$—tarsus $2\frac{2}{10}$—middle toe with claw $1\frac{7}{10}$—tarsus thin, pale yellow, with the anterior and posterior scales each of one entire piece, and no lateral scales. In this specimen too the head and back of neck are darkest, almost black indeed, and the tail light grey with four broad dark bars on the centre feathers and six on the external ones, face and ears dusky, throat white, with longitudinal medial stripe—and under tail-coverts pure white. I possess a drawing of this bird, but am at present unwilling to separate it from the *Besra* till I am more thoroughly certified of the changes of plumage the latter undergoes, and especially the style of the markings of the lower plumage. Native Falconers enumerate several varieties of the *Besra,* some of which may be distinct species, others perhaps only varieties of colour. These I shall allude to presently.

Two other well ascertained species of Sparrow Hawk are found in the South of India, one the *Accip. Dussumierii F. Dussumierii* of Temminck, the *Acc. Dukhunensis* of

Sykes, and probably also *F. badius* figured most wretchedly in Brown's Illustrations of Zoology from Ceylon. This is the *Shikra* of the Natives, is well known and extremely common, and is more frequently trained than any other bird of prey in India. It is a bold, though not a very speedy bird, yet will seize partridges or quails, and strike down a crow or even a larger bird. I see that Mr. Blyth proposes placing it in the genus *Astur,* rather than in *Accipiter,* owing to the shortness of its toes, but though this character certainly makes it an aberrant species of the latter genus, its superior length of tarsus would equally make it an aberrant *Astur.* The other Hawk is closely allied to the European *Acc. fringillarius.* It is the BASHA of Indian Falconry, and has been named *Acc. nisosimilis* by Lieut. Tickell of the Bengal Army. The *Khandesra* is another small species which I have hitherto in vain endeavoured to procure, though the concurrent testimony of many Shikaries from all parts of the country gives me every reason to conclude that it is a distinct and well marked species. It was described to me as having a shade of plumage more resembling the *Basha* than the *Besra,* with the markings small and ill defined, a small head and eye, and a short tail—and is about the size of the *Besra.* It is said to be the speediest of all the Sparrow Hawks. I trust to be enabled to procure one before very long.

In a Native work on Falconry, I saw at Aurungabad, the *Besra* is enumerated, and four varieties are mentioned—1st, The *Khandesra*—2nd, The *Chateesrah*—3rd, The *Sakhurtah,* and 4th, The *Besra* proper—of these I have already mentioned the *Besra* and the *Khandesra.* I have also heard Falconers speak of the *Chateesrah* but it appears little known at present, and the *Sukhurtah* appears unknown now. In another work sent to me by Mr. Blyth for perusal, the *Besra* is thus divided.—1st, The *Khund Besra* probably the same as the *Khandesra.*—2nd, *Khura Besra,* perhaps the *Besra* proper.—3rd, The *Jutesura,* most likely the *Chateesrah.*—4th, *Bhagureena*—this I never heard of—it may be a native synonym of the *Sukhurtah.*—5th, *Khôd.*—6th, *Khur Besra.*—7th, *Manik Besra.* I strongly suspect that these three names are only different appellations for the same hawk which from the description given of the *Manik Besra* is undoubtedly the *Astur Indicus* of Hodgson, called *Gôr Besra* in the South of India, which is also again mentioned shortly afterwards in the same work as the *Chooryalee,* a name which Hodgson in his description of *Astur Indicus* gives as its name in the Eastern Tarai.

I trust to be enabled in the course of the present series of Illustrations to give a drawing of the second plumage of the *Besra* from a living specimen.

V

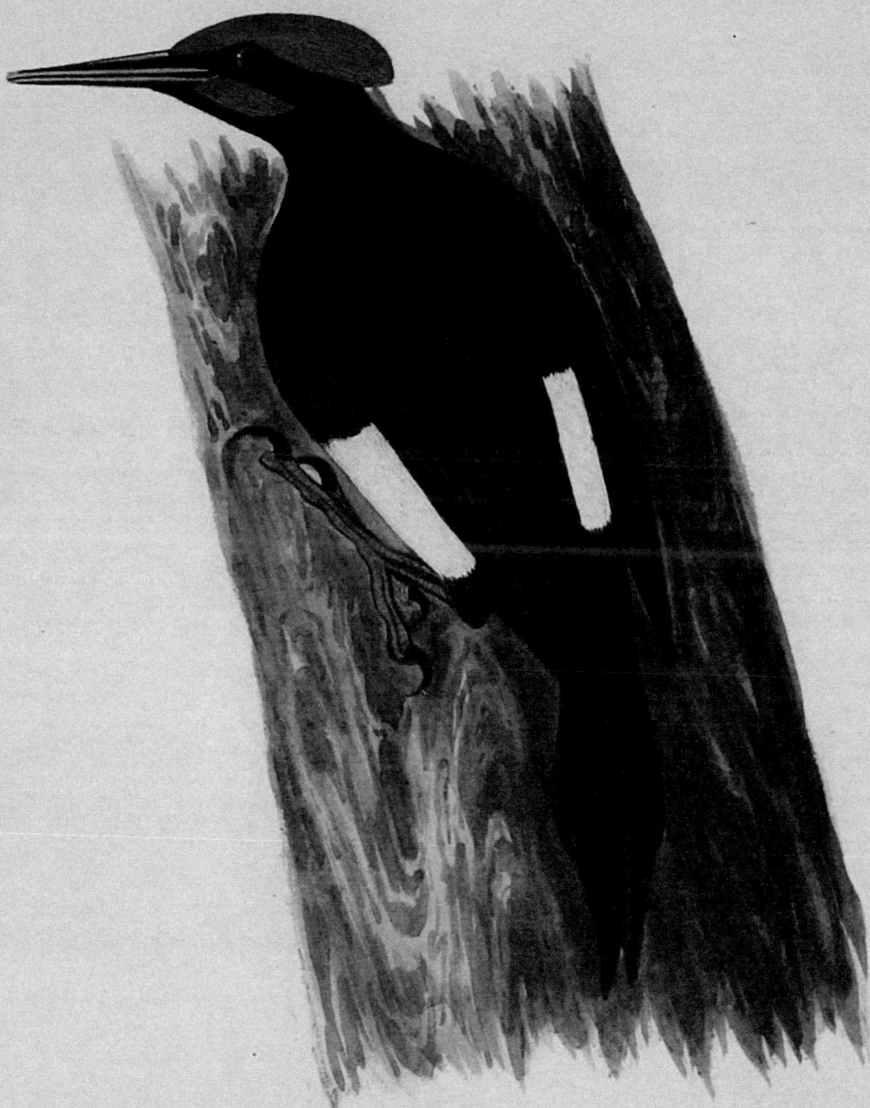

Picus Hodgsonii,

Painted by C.V. Kistnarajoo,

ORD. INSESSORES.

TRIBE—SCANSORES.

FAM. PICIDÆ.

GEN. PICUS.

PLATE V.

PICUS HODGSONII—Jerdon.

WHITE-BACKED WOODPECKER.

Synon.—*Hemilophus Hodgsonii,* Jerdon, No. 213, Cat. (with coloured figure) Madras Journ. of Lit. and Science, No. XXVII, page 215.

This fine *Woodpecker* is found in the lofty forests of Western India, but is by no means common, and I have never yet been enabled to procure a fresh specimen, as it is extremely wary. Native Shikarees however occasionally shoot it, and it is by no means uncommon to see it in collections formed by Gentlemen on the West coast. Of its geographical distribution out of the Peninsula, I am at present ignorant.

Description.—Head, crest, and stripe from the lower mandible crimson, lower part of the back and middle of the belly white, the rest of the plumage deep black, bill black, legs plumbeous. Length of one specimen (the largest I have seen) $19\frac{1}{2}$ inches long—of wing 9—tail $7\frac{1}{2}$—tarsus $1\frac{1}{2}$—bill to front $2\frac{3}{10}$—at gape $2\frac{8}{10}$—width at base $\frac{1}{2}$ inch—wing with 6th quill longest—tail much wedged. It appears to belong to Swainson's subgenus *Hemilophus*.

It appears to resemble very closely the *Picus lencogaster* of Temminck, which Horsfield identifies with his *P. Javensis,* since named *P. Horsfieldii* by Wagler. In none of the descriptions however of these species do I find any mention of the conspicuously white back. Mr. Blyth however seems to think that my bird may be identical with *leuco-gaster,* as he has seen a specimen of this latter from the Tenasserim Coast with some white on the lower part of its back,—but as I have now seen some six or eight specimens of *P. Hodgsonii,* in each of which the white back was equally developed, I am therefore led to conclude that it is a distinct species. I beg to repeat here that I have very great pleasure in dedicating this fine *Woodpecker* to B. H. Hodgson, Esq., our accomplished Resident at the Court of Nepal, whose long promised work on the Zoology of that country, I am glad to see may shortly be expected.

Prinia cursitans,

Painted by C.V. Kostmarijer.

ORD. INSESSORES.

TRIBE—DENTIROSTRES.

FAM. SYLVIADE.

GENUS PRINIA.

PLATE VI.

PRINIA CURSITANS—*Franklin.*

GRASS WARBLER.

THIS curiously plumaged little species of *Prinia* was first described by Major Franklin in his excellent Catalogue of Birds before alluded to. Since this plate was printed, Mr. Blyth has suggested to me that it would be more appropriately included in the genus *Cysticola* of modern authors. It appears to have a very extended distribution over the Continent of India, being found from the Himalayas to Cape Comorin, within a few miles of which place I first procured it. I have seen it in every district where I have been and at all levels up to the summit of the Neilgherries. It is only found in long grass, or corn and rice fields, and is a permanent resident here. On being raised it will occasionally take refuge in a low tree or bush, if such shelter happen to be close at hand, but in general it flies slowly, in a jerking manner and with apparent difficulty for a few yards, and then drops down and conceals itself among the blades of grass or corn, allowing you to approach very close, before it again attempts to rise. It often advances rapidly several yards from the spot where it alighted, but whether by running on the ground (as its name would seem to imply) or by hopping from blade to blade I cannot say.

The *Grass Warbler* feeds on ants, larvæ of grasshoppers, and various other small insects. I have not succeeded in finding its nest, but have been told that it lays its eggs on the ground in a tuft of grass. It is far from being an uncommon bird, and most Sportsmen whether after snipe, florikin, or quail must have flushed hundreds of them. The Hindustani name signifies *Grass Warbler,* the word *Phootkee,* or *Pitpittee,* being applied indiscriminately to all the small *Priniæ* and *Sylviæ,* in this case however with a distinct specific appellation indicative of its resorts.

Description—Plumage above of a pale yellowish brown, largely streaked with dark brown—chin and throat white, the rest of the plumage beneath pale fulvous or rufescent—tail feathers (except the two centre ones) with a black band at the apex, tipped white—this is most strongly marked beneath—quills and centre tail feathers dusky edged with brown—bill brown, pale beneath—legs fleshy yellow—irides light brownish yellow. Length 4 to $4\frac{1}{4}$ inches—wing $1\frac{8}{10}$—2—tail nearly 2—arsus $\frac{8}{10}$—extent of wings $5\frac{1}{4}$—bill at front $\frac{7}{20}$.

VII

Muscipeta paradisea,

Printed by Litho CV Kistnarajoo,

ORD. INSESSORES.

TRIBE—DENTIROSTRES.

FAM. MUSCICAPIDÆ.

GENUS MUSCIPETA.

PLATE VII.

MUSCIPETA PARADISEA.

PARADISE FLYCATCHER.

Synon.—*Muscicapa paradisi,* L.—*M. Indica,* Stephens.—*Upupa paradisea,* L.—*M. castanea,* Temm.

I HAVE introduced here a drawing of this well known *Flycatcher,* to prove the fact that the *Muscipeta Indica* and *M. paradisea* of authors are one and the same species. This I presume has been suspected more or less by various Naturalists, for Colonel Sykes in his Catalogue of Birds of the Dukkun* speaking of these two supposed species, says, "These two birds have been lately erroneously considered to belong to one species. They were never found, however, by Colonel Sykes (who shot many) in the same locality, nor did he observe any intermediate state of plumage. The difference between the females of the two birds at once decides the distinction of species." For my own part though I recognised the exact identity of size and structure, I never doubted that Colonel Sykes was correct in his assertion, until I met with the specimen, a figure of which is here given. Knowing the interest attached to such a specimen, I sent it to Mr. Blyth for inspection, and that gentleman in his Report of the Asiatic Society's Museum for September 1842, makes the following observations on it. "A particularly interesting specimen, as demonstrating what I have for some time been convinced of from observation of the living birds,

* Proceedings of Zoological Society for 1832, page 84.

and especially their notes, that this and the *M. Indica vel castanea* Auctorum, are but different states of plumage of the same species, both sexes of which attain the white garb with full maturity, though breeding before they assume this livery. In the present specimen, a male, which is sent for inspection and exhibition by Mr. Jerdon, the whole under parts, some of the upper tail-coverts, and the upper tertiaries of the wings are pure white, the last displaying the usual black markings, while the rest of the plumage is bright chesnut, except the head and neck, which are glossy green-black as usual, and it moreover does not appear that this bird was moulting, but that the individual had thrown out this intermediate garb at the last renewal of its feathers, a few of these (among the interscapularies) being partly white, and partly of the chesnut hue of reputed *M. castanea*. One of our taxidermists assures me, however, that he has shot a male of this species during its moult, in which the chesnut feathers were all being replaced by white ones, and mentions particularly that one only of its long chesnut middle tail-feathers had been cast; and that a new white one was growing in its place. I may further add that Mr. Hodgson has already presented the Museum with white and chesnut specimens, referring both to *M. paradisea*; and that I have seen a white male paired with a chesnut female, though more frequently pairs of the same colour associate. This bird is not uncommon in the vicinity of Calcutta at all seasons; and I have seen a nest of young ones which were dull chesnut, with merely a slight indication of the black hood."* On writing to my friend S. N. Ward, Esq. M. C. S. on this subject he seems to think (and he has had good opportunity of observing these birds) that the whiteplumaged birds, are males in their breeding plumage only, and that they change back to their usual chesnut hue afterwards, also that the females are always red. That this latter is the case I have always been led to believe (never having shot a white female) in opposition to Mr. Blyth's idea that "both sexes attain the white garb with full maturity." Further investigations are still wanting to enable us to come at the whole truth.

This elegant *Flycatcher* is dispersed over the whole continent of India, but is only at all common in the most wooded portions of the country, preferring dense bamboo jungle. It however occasionally visits gardens and groves of trees in all parts of the Peninsula. In its habits it is restless and wandering, flitting continually from branch to branch, and often wandering from tree to tree. It feeds on various insects which it captures in the air, or occasionally snaps off a branch. Colonel Sykes says, it feeds in the ground, and chiefly on very minute insects. This I have not found to be the case as far as my opportunities of ob-

* Journal Asiatic Society, No. 129, page 884.

serving this bird have served. I have generally seen it single, occasionally in pairs. It is said to breed in bamboos. It has a loud harsh grating cry of alarm, but I never heard any other note. When it seizes an insect it makes a loud snap with its mandibles.

I need not give a further description of the *Paradise Flycatcher,* and shall merely here add its dimensions. Length to end of ordinary tail about 9 inches—wing $3\frac{9}{10}$—tail about 5, centre tail feathers vary from 14 to 21 inches or more—bill at front $\frac{7}{10}$ths—at gape $1\frac{1}{10}$th—tarsus $\frac{7}{10}$ths—bill and orbits lilac blue—inside of mouth pale yellow—legs and feet pale blueish—irides dark brown. Mr. Ward informs me that he lately procured a white male with 3 long tail feathers.

Its name in Hindustanee is *Hoosseinee Bulbul* (the white one) and *Shah Bulbul* or *Sultana Bulbul* (the chesnut one.) In Teloogoo it is called *Tonka Peegeelee-pitta,* which means long tailed Bulbul, and in Tamool, *Walkondalatee,* which has the same meaning. In Malyalum I was informed it is called by a name signifying the king of heaven.

VIII

Turdus wardii.

Printed by Litho. C.V. Kistnarajoo.

ORD. INSESSORES.

TRIBE—DENTIROSTRES.

FAM. MERULIDÆ.

GENUS TURDUS.

PLATE VIII.

TURDUS WARDII—*Jerdon.*

PIED THRUSH.

I am indebted to my friend S. N. Ward, Esq. M. C. S., for the only specimen of this curious *Thrush,* I have yet seen. It was procured by him in the table-land of Mysore immediately below the Segoor pass of the Neilgherries, during the cool season—I regret that I know nothing of its habits.

I have dedicated it to Mr. Ward a keen and zealous Naturalist to whose researches I am already indebted for several novelties, and from whom I hope to receive shortly a still further accession to the Peninsular Fauna. Mr. Blyth to whom I forwarded for inspection the unique specimen I possess of this *Thrush,* thus speaks of it in his Museum report for September 1842. " A remarkably coloured species from Mysore, connecting the Blackbird group with the *Oreocinclæ* of Gould."

Description.—General colour black—eye-streak and lower parts from the breast white—upper tail coverts banded black and white, all the wing feathers tipped white, forming a conspicuous patch on the lesser wing coverts, a streak on the edge of the greater coverts, and another on the end of the smaller wing feathers. Sides of the body banded with dusky black—tail feathers black, white tipped and edged, most so on the external feathers, diminishing to the medial tail feathers—irides dark brown —bill yellow, dusky at the base above—legs, feet and claws yellow. Length 9 inches—extent $14\frac{1}{3}$—wing from flexure $4\frac{6}{10}$—tail $3\frac{2}{10}$—tarsus $1\frac{3}{10}$ to sole—bill at gape $1\frac{2}{10}$—to forehead $\frac{8\frac{1}{2}}{10}$ths. Weighed nearly $2\frac{1}{2}$ oz.—third quill longest—second equal to the fifth—first rudimentary—fourth very slightly shorter than the third.

Scolopax nemoricola.

Printed by Litho. C.V. Kistnarojoo

ORD. GRALLATORES.

FAM. SCOLOPACIDÆ.

GENUS SCOLOPAX.

PLATE IX.

SCOLOPAX NEMORICOLA—Hodgson.

WOOD SNIPE—Do.

THIS bird, the solitary *Snipe* of Sportsmen on the Neilgherries, is a cold weather visitant to those hills, and probably also to other of the elevated table-lands of Southern India, as well as to the summit of the wooded ghauts. I have been informed that several large or 'solitary snipe' have been shot at times in different parts of the low country, which most likely were of this species. Mr. Hodgson first described* this *Snipe* as a winter resident in Nepal. Of its geographical range out of India we have at present no information, but it probably extends far North, and likewise towards the East.

On the Neilgherries the *solitary Snipe* is by no means abundant, seldom more than two or three dozens being in general shot during the whole season. It frequents the skirts of the dense woods on the hills, generally near a swamp or marshy ground, or a running stream, and is never flushed in the open ground, and when driven from a wood always seeks the shelter of a bush if no other wood be at hand. It seldom flies to any distance, taking advantage of the nearest available place of refuge. Its flight is not very rapid and indeed rather heavy. Though so little larger than the common Snipe, its broad wings give it more the appearance of a Woodcock on the wing, for which it is invariably mistaken by a beginner.

* Gleanings of Science, No. 32—and Journal Asiatic Society, Vol. vi, page 490.

Description.—I shall here content myself with saying that it differs in coloring from the *common Snipe* chiefly in the whole of the under surface being barred. Other shades of difference will be better appreciated by comparing a common Snipe with the figure here given, than by the most elaborate description.

Dimensions.—Length about $12\frac{1}{2}$ to 13 inches long—extent 19—of wing $5\frac{1}{2}$—T. $2\frac{1}{2}$—bill $2\frac{6}{10}$—tarsus $1\frac{1}{2}$—I have generally found them about $5\frac{1}{2}$ ounces heavy ; Mr. Hodgson says, weight 7 oz.

I shall here transcribe part of Mr. Hodgson's remarks on this bird. " This interesting species forms by its size, its manners, and some points of its structure, a link between the genera *Scolopax*, and *Gallinago*, but deviates from both towards *Rhynchæa*, by the feebleness of its soft, bowed and sub-gradated wings which have the second quill longest. Its general structure is that of a *Snipe*, but its bill is a Woodcock's, and the legs and feet are larger than in *Gallinago*. It is shy, non-gregarious, avoids the open cultivated country, and is only found in the haunts of the Woodcock, with this difference in its manners, as compared with those of *Scolopax*, that it is averse from the interior of woods. The wings are usually from $\frac{3}{4}$ to 1 inch less than the tail, and the prime and tertial quills are equal. The tarsi differ from those of the common Snipe in that the scales, posteally are broken on the mesial line, whereas they are entire in that bird."

Pterocles quadricinctus

Printed by Litho Cl. Kistnarajoo

ORD. RASORES.

FAM. TETRAONIDÆ.

GEN.] PTEROCLES.

PLATE X.

PTEROCLES QUADRICINCTUS.

PAINTED ROCK GROUSE.

MALE.

Synon.—*Ptorocles quadricinctus*, Temminck, Pig. et Gall? *Gelinote des Indes*—Sonnerat —*Tetrao Indicus,* Gmelin—*Perdix Indica,* Latham—*Ænas Indicus* and *Æ. bicinctus* of Vieillot (according to Lesson and Wagler.)

If the *Pterocles quadricinctus* of Temminck, an inhabitant of Senegambia, be identical with our Indian *painted Rock-grouse,* as is asserted in all the systematic works I have access to, which give both Africa and India as its habitat, than the specific name *Indicus,* long ago employed, has the priority; but, on comparing specimens lately with Wagler's description, I found several points of difference, and Wagler himself says, 'Is the bird described by Sonnerat really to be referred to this?' Had I noted this sooner, and before the Plate was printed, I would have been inclined to have substituted the old term *Indicus,* but as our Indian bird had been referred without any hesitation to *quadricinctus* by Colonel Sykes, as well as by all systematists, I omitted previously to compare it more accurately. As it is, I am now inclined to consider our present *Rock-grouse* a distinct species from *Quadricinctus,* and it will of course bear the name of *Pterocles Indicus.*

This handsomely plumaged *Rock-grouse* is to be found in suitable localities throughout India, but is by no means a common or abundant species. Unlike the *Pterocles exustus,* which delights in the bare and rocky plains, this bird is only to be seen in bushy and jungly ground, and prefers the neighbourhood of low hills. It is always met with in pairs, and when flushed, rises with a low chuckling call, takes a very short flight and alights. It sometimes, if followed, runs a short distance, and it is raised again with great difficulty. Its food consists of various hard seeds, and the Natives invariably assert that both this and the common *Rock-grouse* feed on gravel alone. It breeds during the hot weather laying two or three eggs of an olive colour, speckled with spots of olive brown and dusky, and of a long cylindrical shape, equally rounded at both ends. Its flesh is delicate and well flavoured. Though it does not occur in sufficient numbers to induce the Sportsman to follow it alone, yet in beating the low jungles for other game, a pair or two are occasionally flushed and shot. This bird and the *Pterocles exustus* are known to Sportsmen in India by the name of *Rock-pigeon,* our present species being distinguished by the epithet *painted,* as indicative of the beauty of its markings. In Hindustani they are named *Burtoetur,* the subject of our Plate being called by some *Hundeyree.* In Teloogoo, they are called *Polunkar,* and in Tamool, *Kul Koudaree* or *Rock-partridge.*

Description—Male—Forehead and sinciput pure white, with a broad black band between. Back of head rufous yellow with black stripes—neck, breast and lesser wing coverts of a pale tawny yellow, shaded with a greenish hue. Three bands on the breast, the first marroon, the second pale yellowish, and the last dark chocolate—the feathers of the rest of the lower plumage banded dark chocolate brown and pale yellowish—plumage above banded dark brown and rufous yellow ; the larger wing coverts rufous yellow at the tip, then with a band of a dusky or inky hue, next a white one, and then another fainter inky one on a pale dusky yellow ground, this last inky band being sometimes edged by another narrow white one. Quills dusky, edged with yellow—tail banded brown and yellow—bill red—orbitar skin pale lemon yellow—irides deep brown—legs and feet ochreous yellow.

Length about 10 inches—wing 7¼—tail 3—extent of wings nearly 21 inches—weight about 7 ounces.

I intend to give a figure of the Female bird in a future number of the Illustrations.

XI

Phœnicornis flammeus,

Printed by Litho. C.V. Kistnarajoo,

ORD. INSESSORES.

TRIBE—DENTIROSTRES.

FAM. LANIADÆ.

SUB-FAM. CEBPLEPYRINE.

GEN. PHÆNICORNIS.

PLATE XI.

PHÆNICORNIS FLAMMEUS.

FIERY-RED BIRD.

MALE AND FEMALE.

Synon.—*Muscicapa flammea,* Temm. P. C. 263—*M. Subflava,* Vieillot? *Gobe mouche oranor de l'Isle de Ceylon,* Levaillant?

Sayelee—Hindustani.

The genus *Phænicornis* was separated by Swainson, and is a very distinct and well characterized group of birds. I see, however, that Mr. Gray, in his Genera of Birds, considers Boie's genus *Pericrocotus* to be synonymous and to have the priority. As however Swainson's name has now been in considerable use in this country, and as there are still some doubts as to the exact identity of several of these supposed synonymous genera, I have for the present retained our countryman's name till a Committee of Ornithologists has finally fixed on the name and limits of each genus, and till the names imposed by our own Naturalists, when they have a prior claim, are fully acknowledged by Foreigners.

This handsome bird is a denizen of all the large forests of Southern India. I have seen it in Travancore, Malabar, the Wynaad, and the forest skirting the base of the Neilgherries on its Eastern face, but not in the Carnatic or Deccan, there being no forests in these districts, except here and there on the slope, and at the base of the Eastern ghauts, and in the places where I have traversed these hills, I have looked in vain for it. Towards the North of the Peninsula, in the jungles of Goomsoor, its place is occupied by the *Phœnicornis princeps* and *P. brevirostris* of Vigors, which two species appear to extend through Central India to the Himalayas. The *Phœnicornis flammeus,* though often to be seen in the more open and cleared spaces of the jungles, is never, that I have observed met with away from the woods. It ascends the sides of mountain ranges to a considerable height, and I fancied was more numerous in the elevated region of Wynaad, than in most other localities. I saw it though rarely in woods on the summit of the Neilgherries, but only at their Northern face. It is a tolerably common and abundant species in its appropriate haunts, and, from its bright and showy colours, attracts the notice of most travellers through the lofty forests of Western India.

It keeps chiefly to the tops of high trees, where it may be seen usually in small flocks, frisking about, picking an insect off a branch or leaf, or occasionally catching one in the air. The males keep up a continual whistling call. Its food seems to consist chiefly of coleopterous insects.

The *Gobe mouche oranor de l'Isle de Ceylon* figured by Levaillant in his Oiseaux d'Afrique, Plate 155, and named *Subflava* by Vieillot, appears to me to be very probably this species, though I see that Lesson refers it to his genus *Muscylva,* and makes it synonymous with Gmelin's *Rufiventer,* while *M. miniata,* and *M. flammea* are referred to his genus *Acis* which is the same I believe as *Phœnicornis.* Should this conjecture be correct, *Subflava ,* would have the priority of *flammea* I suppose, unless indeed the *Ph. flammeus* of Swainson, or Temminck's *M. flammea* prove distinct from the species of Southern India, figured here, which I suspect may be the case, as Mr. Blyth informs me that the *P. flammeus* figured in Swainson's Zoological Illustrations, appears to differ somewhat from my specimens of presumed *flammeus.*

I can add nothing to the knowledge to be gained from an examination of the accompanying Plate, except by giving the dimensions of the bird which are as follows.

Length 8 to $8\frac{1}{2}$ inches,—wing $3\frac{7}{10}$—tail 4,—tarsus $\frac{8}{10}$,—bill at front $\frac{4}{10}$ths.

Besides *P. princeps,* and *P. brevirostris* of Vigors, previously mentioned as having been procured by me in Goomsoor, there are others found on the Continent of India which I shall briefly enumerate here.

Phœnicornis Flammeus.

Phœnicornis roseus—*Muscicapa rosea* Vieillot, N. D. d'Hist. Nat. 21, p. 486. I had considered this bird as the young of *flammeus* or *brevirostris,* although I recognised some peculiarities of structure, but Mr. Blyth first pointed out to me its distinctness. It is found in the neighbourhood of Calcutta and I obtained it in Goomsoor, and have seen specimens from Malabar.

P. peregrinus—*Parus peregrinus* and *Parus Malabaricus* Auctorum—*Sat'h Sayelee* H.

This well known little bird is more generally spread than any of the genus, and instead of being confined to forests, is often to be met with in low jungle, gardens, and avenues in all parts of the country.

A sixth Continental species perhaps exists in the *Muscicapa erythropygia,* No. 156 of my Catalogue, though its more depressed bill, weaker legs and feet, and the mode of variation in the female led me to class it as a *Flycatcher,* and in the same group as *M. picata* of Sykes, wrongly referred by me to *M. hirundinacea* of Temminck. In its colours the male resembles most of the species of *Phœnicornis,* except in having a white stripe on the wings, and in some of the tail feathers. The female differs from the male in having ashy brown instead of glossy black, and cinereous white, where the male has bright orange red. The irides also are light coloured; but notwithstanding these slight deviations, I am inclined to agree with Mr. Blyth, who first called my attention to the subject, and consider it as a species of *Phœnicornis.*

Another species of this genus, the *P. miniata* of authors to which Swainson, erroneously I imagine, refers *P. brevirostris,* is said by Lesson to have been sent from Bengal, but it was originally described from Java I believe, and is most probably a species peculiar to the Malayan countries.

I am indebted to my friend Mr. Ward for the sketch from which this drawing was made.

Falco Shaheen
young male,

Printed by C.V. Hastumajee.
1843

ORD. RAPTORES.

TRIBE—FALCONIDÆ.

FAM. FALCONINÆ.

GEN. FALCO.

PLATE XII.

FALCO SHAHEEN.

THE SHAHEEN FALCON.

YOUNG MALE.

Synon.---*Falco Shaheen,* Jerdon, Madras Journal of Literature and Science XXIV.---Catal. No. 29.---*F. Aldrovandi* of the Supplement to my Catal., not *F. Aldrovandi* of Temminck ---*F. Sultaneus,* Hodgson MSS.—*F. Ruber Indicus,* Brisson Encyclop. Method. page 129.

Shaheen in Hindustani, the male *Koela—Jawolum* in Teloogoo, *Wulloor* in Tamool.

THIS fine falcon was I believe first noticed by myself in the Catalogue of Indian Birds above alluded to, and the Hindustani name affixed to it as a specific one. Mr. Hodgson, though he has not described it, lately sent it to the Museum at Calcutta, under the manuscript name of *Sultaneus,* which, being, as it were, a Latin translation of the native name, I would have adopted had I not previously had my own name printed on the Plate. I learn also from Mr. Blyth, that it was long ago known to and figured by Buchanan. Mr. Elliot in a note to my description of the *Shaheen,* says, that he considered it to be the *Falco Aldrovandi* of Temminck, which is the *F. severus* of Horsfield, and accordingly, in the Supplement to my Catalogue, I referred to it under that name, stating that the size as given in Griffith's Cuvier had misled me, for that otherwise the description appeared to large falcon used by the natives, which, being of a more patient and docile disposition, will stay up above an hour.

In the works on Falconry I have before alluded to, the name *Shaheen* is said to be that by which it is known in Persia, as well as among the Mussulmen of India. *Kohee* being the name given it by the Hindoos of the North of India, whence, in all probability, comes the name of the male bird in general use, viz. *Koela,* or *Kohela,*—though it is said to be called *Shaheen Bucha* in Persia. It is said to bear the name of *Laheen* in Toorkistan, and *Kubursh* in Arabic. Among the localities for it given in the Native works of falconry are Koordistan, Khorasan, Moultan and Cabool. Several varieties are enumerated viz. the red, the white, the blue, and the black, but these are merely shades of difference in the colours and in the more or less distinctness of the markings. These variations, however, I may remark, are very considerable in this falcon, as well as in the peregrines found in India, and are probably in some measure owing to the long domestication, if I may so speak, of these birds, as it is well known that birds moulting in confinement vary somewhat in the shades of their plumage from those subject to the more vigorous actions of a wild state of life.

Description.—I shall here content myself with giving a description of the young *Shaheen,* and a very brief account of its changes, as I am waiting for further information on the subject, and purpose giving in a future Plate, a figure of the adult bird, when I will add a fuller and more accurate account of its changes of plumage than I am at present enabled to give.

Young Male—Plumage above generally of a dark cinereous, or dusky blackish hue, darkest on the head, hind neck and cheek stripe—most of the feathers are narrowly edged with rufous, those on the lower part of the back and rump more broadly so. There is some rufous on the forehead, and on the back of the head where it forms a sort of crucial mark. Tail paler than the rest of the body, faintly barred with rufous, and tipped the same —Chin and throat pale rufous yellow, unspotted—cheeks of the same tint with narrow dark stripes. The rest of the plumage beneath bright rufous or chesnut, with longitudinal dark brown markings on the centre of the body, oblong spots on the sides, and arrow shaped markings on the lower part of the abdomen. Under wing coverts rufous barred with brown; quills, barred with rufous on their inner webs. Bill blueish, darker at the tip —cere and orbitar skin pale yellow—irides dark brown—legs and feet yellow. Length 15 inches—wing 11—tail 5½—tarsus nearly 2—centre toe and claw ½2—weight 1lb.

A young female I had alive at the same time as the one from which the above description was taken, differed from the male in having the chin, throat and cheeks white, in the rufous edgings to the feathers being very indistinct, and the plumage generally being of a darker hue.

Length of a female 17½ to 18 inches—weight 1lb., 10oz.

After the first moult, the markings of the lower surface disappear, except a few on the lower part of the abdomen and leg feathers, the plumage above becomes more of a blueish tinge, and the edgings and barrings disappear—with further moultings the shade of the plumage above becomes still lighter, and of a slaty blue, the markings beneath vanish entirely, and the rufous tint of the breast becomes paler.

The accompanying figure was taken from a living bird I had for some time in my possession at Madras.

ADDENDUM.

The *Falco guttatus* of G. R. Gray, recently* described in the *Annals and Magazine of Natural History*, vol. 11, page 371, appears to me to be identical with, or at all events very closely allied to, my *Falco Shaheen*. It is from the Phillipine Islands.

* May 1843.

XIII

Crateropus Delessertii,

Printed by Litho C.V. Kistnarajoo,

ORD. INSESSORES.

FAM. CRATEROPODINÆ.

GEN. CRATEROPUS.

PLATE XIII.

CRATEROPUS DELESSERTI.

WHITE BREASTED BABBLER.

Synon.—*C. Delesserti,* Jerdon—Madras Journal Literature and Science, No. 25 Catal. No. 88. *C. Griseiceps*—Delessert.

THE genus *Crateropus* of Swainson appears to have been first defined by M. Lesson as *Garrulax**, and has also, though subsequently to Swainson's definition, received the name of *Xanthocincla* from Mr. Gould.—In my catalogue of Indian Birds published in the Madras Journal I ventured to join these three synonyms, and I see that they have been generally recognised as identical; but the name given by Lesson has been preferred, having been bestowed prior to the others, and the late rules acted on by Gray, Strickland and others have enforced this has the first law of Zoological nomenclature.

The white breasted Babbler was first named by myself in the Catalogue before alluded to from a single specimen obtained by M. Delessert whilst collecting on the Neilgherries, and which that Gentleman kindly lent me for inspection. Mr. Blyth informs me that in the Revue Zoologique, 1840—and in the 'Souvenirs de voyage dans L' Inde' published by M. Delessert, subsequently to the appearance of my Catalogue, this species is described as C. *Griseiceps.*—I have never myself been fortunate enough to procure a specimen, but Lord Arthur Hay, a most zealous and enthusiastic naturalist has very recently obtained one, which he shot on the Coonoor Ghaut of the Neilgherries.

The species of this genus appear to be chiefly confined to the wooded regions of Northern India, and the countries to the Eastward, and no less than 30 species are recorded

* Traite d' Ornithologie—1831—page 647.

A

by Vigors, Gould, Hodgson, Blyth and others, as inhabitants of the Himalayas and neighbouring countries, whilst this and my *Crateropus Cachinnans* are the only hitherto recorded species of Southern India.—Mr. Blyth remarks the close affinity of our present subject to *C. Gularis.*

The manners of the *C. Cachinnans,* the only member of this group I have myself observed, are something smilar to those of the other genera of this family, but much less social than the Malacocirci, which are apparently the most typical of the group. The Laughing Thrush is sometimes seen in small flocks, but often wanders about alone, though at no great distance from some of its species, with whom it continually keeps up a noisy communication as signal of the direction it is going, or of the abundance of food obtained. It inhabits the densest woods on the summits of the Neilgherries, keeping chiefly to the lower branches of trees and brushwood, and feeds principally on fruit especially on the pleasant fruit of the Brazil cherry (Physalis tomentosa), now so abundant in most of the woods in the neighbourhood of Ootacamund.—It also occasionally feeds on caterpillars and other soft bodied insects.

I have no doubt that our present species has some what similar manners, indeed Lord A. Hay informs me "that it has much the same skulling habits as the C. Cachinnans."

The nidification of any of the *Crateropi* has not that I am aware been yet recorded. On one occasion only I found the nest of *C. Cachinnans* on a bank overhanging the road on the top of the Nediwuttum Ghaut of the Neilgherries—It was made of roots, grass and moss, and contained 4 long oval pure white eggs. I shall now add a description of the *C. Delesserti.*

Description.—Head and nape dusky black—rest of the plumage above dark rufous, growing brighter on the upper tail coverts—chin, throat and breast white, edged with grey—belly and vent bright rufous—Tail brownish black, brown at the base of the feathers—Bill dusky above—yellow beneath—legs pale reddish—Length $10\frac{1}{2}$—11 inch—wing $4\frac{2}{10}$—Tail $4\frac{1}{2}$—Bill (front) 1—Tarsus $1\frac{1}{2}$.—Irides red.

Muscicapa albicaudata,

Printed by Litho. G.V. Kistnaryso,

ORD. INSESSORES.

FAM. MUSCICAPIDÆ.

GEN. MUSCICAPA.

PLATE XIV.

MUSCICAPA ALBICAUDATA. *Jerdon.*

NEILGHERRY BLUE FLYCATCHER.

Synon.—*M. albicaudata Jerdon*, Catal. No. 152.

The genus Muscicapa, even as restricted by Cuvier, has of late been considerably subdivided, and when we consider the varied nature of its contents, apparently with benefit to science.

There are in India several Flycatchers, whose prevailing tint is blue, of various shades and intensity, among which more or less structural differences exist. These Mr. Blyth divides into several groups, each of which has one or more representative in Southern India. *Muscicapa banyumas* of Horsfield, together with my *M. pallipes*, Cat. No. 149, and three or four species from Northern India, Mr. B. classes under the name of *Cyornis*;* my *M. superciliaris* Cat. No. 153, together with one or two more very pretty diminutive species he classes as *Muscicapula*;* whilst the subject of the acccompanying plate with *M. Melanops*, and I think also *M Indigo* of Horsfield, constitute his genus *Stoparola*. They differ generally from the other blue Flycatchers of India in their more stout and robust habit, stronger legs and feet, and in their bill being shorter, wider at the base, and more depressed, and perhaps also a little more hooked at the tip.

The Neilgherry blue Flycatcher is, as far as it is yet known, confined to the woods on the summit of the Neilgherries, and the forests on the edges of these hills. It occurs in considerable number here, frequenting the higher branches of trees, occasionally seen single,

* Joun. As. Soc. Vol. XII. p. 939.

but not unfrequently in small parties. It is much more restless and active in its habits than the Indian members of the genus *Butalis,* the most fixed and sedentary of all, or of *Cyornis,* flitting about constantly, and changing in its position more frequently than these, indeed more like the *Muscipetæ, Leucocircæ* and *Muscicapa cærulea,* which last has much of the habits of the Fan-tailed Flycatchers. None of these however are seen in groups like the present one, except perhaps now and then the Leucocircæ. I do not remember to have ever heard the note of the Neilgherry blue Flycatcher. I discovered its nest twice, built in a slight hole on a steep earthern bank on a road side, but did not procure the eggs, both birds having forsaken their nests. Its food consists of various insects which it usually takes on the wing, but now and then snaps off a branch.

Description. Of a deep Indigo blue colour, paler on the lower part of the back, and inclining to lazuline on the forehead, and shoulders; belly ashy blue mingled with whitish; under tail-coverts whitish, barred with dusky blue; wings and tail dusky black, the feathers edged with blue, and those of the tail, centre feathers excepted, white at the base; bill and legs black; Irides deep brown. Length 6—$6\frac{1}{2}$ inches Wing $3\frac{2}{10}$ expanse of do $9\frac{1}{2}$, Tail $2\frac{6}{10}$ Tarsus $\frac{8}{10}$th Bill at front $\frac{4}{10}$th. Weighs from 12 to 14 drams, 4th and 5th quills equal and longest.

The female differs from the male in the more sombre and ashy tint of the plumage, and the young male is spotted throughout with pale rufous.

XV

Oriolus sinensis

Printed by Litho C V Kistnargoo;

ORD. INSESSORES.

FAM. MERULIDÆ.

SUB-FAM. ORIOLINÆ.

GEN. ORIOLUS.

PLATE XV.

ORIOLUS INDICUS.

INDIAN BLACK NAPED ORIOLE.

When I first compiled my Catalogue of Indian Birds I inserted *Oriolus chinensis* of authors as a peninsular species on the Authority of Mr. Elliot, that Gentleman having obtained specimens answering the description of that species in the Southern Mahratta country. I have since procured specimens from Malabar and Travancore, and had a drawing of one executed for the present work under the name of *O. sinensis*. I have however lately seen specimens from China and Manilla in the valuable collection of Lord Arthur Hay, and have also compared the description of Vigors' *O. acrorhynchus*, and Swainson's *O. coronatus*, and I am now compelled to conclude that our peninsular species is distinct from both these, and that moreover *acrorhynchus* refers to the true *chinensis*, and *coronatus* to Wagler's, *hippocrepis*. I have therefore given it the appellation of *Indicus*, partly because I consider that the *O. Indicus* of Brisson and others may possibly refer to this though faultily described.

Specimens from Manilla now before me correspond exactly with Vigors' description of his *acrorhynchus*, as well as with the original description of *chinensis* and that by Buffon of '*Le Conliav an*,' and the figure in the Planches Enlumineés. I am therefore led to believe that Mr. Vigors had compared his Manilla bird with specimens from peninsular India, or from some of the isles, which he had considered at the time as true *chinensis.* Our peninsular species differs from the Chinese one in the following particulars. It has a smaller bill, the secondaries are broadly margined with yellow on their external webs, the innermost of these and the tertiaries having the outer web entirely yellow, whilst in *chinensis* these are almost entirely black. The centre tail feathers in our bird are black to their tip, being only faintly margined with yellow, whilst the Chinese one has a broad yellow tip; and the remaining rectrices have the black extending correspondingly further than in *chinensis*; the black ocular mark extends in our bird to the nares, whilst in the Chinese specimens it only extends a little beyond the angle of the mouth; the band too is much narrower on the nape in the Indian bird; the feathers of the back have usually a greenish tinge, and the yellow throughout is less pure and bright than in the Chinese bird; and lastly the tail is considerably shorter. Swainson's *O. coronatus* from Java (as described) differs from our peninsular bird, and also from true *chinensis*, in its smaller size, shorter wings, tail, and tarsus, and in the narrowness of the black nuchal band. Its bill appears to be somewhat larger than in ours, but shorter than in *chinensis*. Wagler's description of *O. hippocrepis,* which he considers the same as *chinensis* auct., corresponds with it in the yellow tips of the centre tail feathers, and with our peninsular bird in having the black ocular band extending to the nares, and in other points. As however his specimens were obtained chiefly from Java and Sumatra, it is most probably Swainson's *coronatus,* with which indeed it agrees in dimensions pretty nearly, as will be seen in the accompanying table I give for the sake of comparison.

NAME.	Total length.	Wing.	Tail.	Bill (front.)	Tarsus.
O. Chinensis—verus vel. acrorhynchus......	$10\frac{1}{2}$	6	$4\frac{1}{2}$	$1\frac{3}{10}$	above 1
O. Indicus—apud Jerdon................	$10\frac{1}{2}$	$6\frac{2}{10}$	4	$1\frac{5}{30}$	barely 1
O Coronatus Sw.......................	$9\frac{1}{2}$	$5\frac{3}{10}$	$3\frac{1}{2}$	$1\frac{2}{10}$	$\frac{8}{10}$ ths.
O. Hippocrepis—Wagler (german. meas.)....	$9\frac{1}{2}$	$5\frac{2}{12}$	$3\frac{3}{4}$		$\frac{10}{12}$ ths.

The three black naped species will then stand thus.

1. *O. chinensis* L., *O. cochinsinensis* Brisson., Le Conliavan Buffon P. E. 570., *O. acrorhynchus* Vigors. Hab. China, Manilla, Cochinchina &c.

2. *O. coronatus* Swainson, *O. hippocrepis* Wagler (synon. except.). Hab. Java Sumatra, Malayana.

3 *O. Indicus* Jerdon Ill. Ind. Orn. pl. xv. (*O. sinensis* on the plate) *O. Indicus* Brisson.

Hab. Continental India.

The habits of this Oriole do not I presume differ much from those of its congeners, except that it appears to be more especially a denizen of the depths of the forests. It is certainly a rare bird. Mr Blyth has not I believe obtained it from northern India as yet, and I do not know how far it may extend out of the peninsula. I need scarcely add anything more descriptive of this bird than what has already been said in comparing it with the allied species. Its bill appears to have been, like the others of its genus, of a lake red colour, and the feet and legs plumbeous. The female appears to differ chiefly in the less vivid tint of the yellow, in the greenish tinge of the back extending further, and in the wings and tail being of a less pure black. The other peninsular species of Oriole are as follows.

1st *O. Kundoo,* Sykes, (the female), and probably *O. galbula* of the same, *O. galbula* var. A., Latham, *O. aureus* apud Jerdon Cat, No. 97, and of Blyth, probably also *O. galbuloides,* Gould, of a list of Birds from the Punjaub and Cashmere. Common Indian Oriole, Mango bird of Residents in India.

This oriole is very common, inhabits the open country in groves, gardens, avenues, &c. It has a loud mellow note and lives chiefly on fruit, and also on soft bodied insects. I once found the nest of this species, it consisted of a cup shaped nest slightly made with fine grass and roots, and suspended from a rather high branch by a few long fibres of the same material apparently as the nest itself; these did not surround the nest but only supported it on two sides. It contained three eggs, white, spotted chiefly at the larger end with large purplish blotches.

2d *O. Melanocephalus,* auct. (*O. Maderaspatensis* auct., and *O.* Mc. *Goshii,* Tickell are young birds,) Black headed Indian Oriole, chiefly found in Southern India in and about forests, but also occasionally in open country, in avenues, gardens, &c.

The orioles are called in Hindustani 'Peeluk,' a name merely signifying yellow bird. In Teloogoo they ara called 'Vanga pandoo,' or Brinjal fruit, the black headed species being sometimes distinguished by the epithet "Konda,' or Hill, Latham I see gives this name, somewhat misspelt, as that of his *O. Maderaspatensis.* The Malyalum name is Magnakee, which I see Latham calls *Magnalki.*

Swainson describes another black headed Oriole from India as *O. Hodsonii,* but neither Mr. Blyth nor myself have yet met with it.

XVI

Ardea nigra.

Printed by Litho. C.W. Kidderpore,

ORD. GRALLATORES.

FAM. ARDEADÆ.

GEN. ARDEA.

PLATE XVI.

ARDEA FLAVICOLLIS. Lath.

YELLOW NECKED BLACK HERON.

Synon.—*A. nigra Vieill—A. picta* Raffl.?

When I procured the only specimen of this handsome Heron that I have as yet obtained, I referred it to *A. nigra* of Vieillot, (without any hesitation) and had a drawing of it lithographed under that name. I did not then imagine that it could have been Latham's *flavicollis*, either from his description, in which it is said to be of a purple brown colour, or from the figure in Gray and Hardwicke, where it is represented as being of a blue colour. Mr. Blyth however assures me that such is the case, and Wagler I see also gives these name as synonyms.

The specimen from which the accompanying figure was taken was procured at Madras. I have never since got another, but Shikarees have told me that they know the bird, and that it is very rare. Mr. Blyth informs me that it has been obtained at Calcutta, and that he has received it from Arracan, China, and other places to the eastward, where it appears to be much more common than here. Horsfield gives it as Javanese, and Mr. Blyth tells me that he considers *A. picta* of Raffles to be the same. Wagler also gives New Holland as its habitat.

I know nothing if its habits. It is said to frequent the more grassy and weedy tanks, and to shun observation. It is too little known here to have a distinct local appellation.

Mr. Blyth considers it as forming a subdivision of *Butor*, or the Bitterns, which conclusion he came to after seeing a fresh specimen.

Description. Top of head, back of neck, body above, and wings, bright glossy green black; beneath dull sooty black, some of the centre feathers of the abdomen partially tinged with buff; a stripe of golden yellow rnns from the lower mandible to the back of the neck about the lower third, where it is gradually lost; chin, throat, and neck beneath, white, variegated with deep chesnut and black, the feathers short at first but gradually lengthening and becoming lanceolate; each feather has the outer barb and tip black, edged with creamy white, and the inner barb chesnut; the chin and throat want the black, and the white is of a purer tinge. A narrow stripe of close set feathers run from the base of the lower mandible to the ear-coverts, black and chesnut coloured, the bases of the feathers being white; the long feathers of the breast are black, edged with white on both sides.

Length 24—25 inches Wing $8\frac{1}{2}$ Tail $2\frac{3}{4}$, Tarsus $2\frac{3}{4}$ Middle toe $2\frac{3}{4}$, Bill (at front) $3\frac{2}{10}$, at gape nearly 4. Bill appears to have been of a dusky reddish brown—Legs dark green.

The plumage of the young bird is described as being of a saturate blue, and in a further stage, I presume, it gets the purplish brown tinge described by Latham. The smoky tinge described by Horsfield, with the tail deep blue, must be a bird in transition plumage.

XVII

R. E. B. lith. prel. lith. Linn. imp.

LANIUS NIGRICEPS.

ORD. INSESSORES.

FAM. LANIADÆ.

GEN. LANIUS.

PLATE XVII.

LANIUS NIGRICEPS.

BLACK-HEADED SHRIKE.

Synon.—*L. antiguanus* Gmel. ' Piegrieche d' Antigue ' Sonnerat voyage, t. 70. Indian Shrike of Latham, No. 31. *L. nigriceps* Franklin. *L. tricolor* Hodgs., Jerdon Catal. No. 51.

When in Goomsoor some years ago I obtained a single specimen of this Shrike, and Mr. Blyth and Lord Arthur Hay have since procured examples from the same locality. At one time Mr. B. was doubtful whether the Himalayan bird was identical with this, as most of the specimens from Northern India had more rufous on the back than those from central India, but he has recently informed me that he now considers them the same. I have not obtained it myself, nor have I seen specimens, from any other part of the peninsula, and I suspect that it does not occur further South than about N. L. 20°. From thence it extends to the Himalayas, and Eastward to Arracan, and probably still further, as Sonnerat's specimens were procured, he alleges, from the Phillippine isles. The name '*Antiguanus,*' (derived from Antigue, a province of Panay, one of these islands) being liable to lead to error, I have retained Franklin's very appropriate name. The black headed Shrike appears to be a more forest haunting species than its congeners, but does not otherwise, that I am aware of, differ in its habits. Like the other Shrikes it descends to the ground for its food, which consists almost wholly of grasshoppers and their larvæ. I have not observed in any of the Indian species the reputed habit of impaling insects on thorns.

Description, Head and hind neck black, middle of back grey ; lower back and rump rufous, which sometimes extends over the greater portion of the back ; wings and tail black, the secondaries and tail feathers (except the centre ones) edged and tipped wih reddish white. Beneath white ; sides of body, and under tail coverts, rufous. Bill and legs black. Irides deep brown. Length about $9\frac{1}{2}$ to 10 inches, wing $3\frac{3}{10}$ Tail 5. Tars $1\frac{1}{10}$.

The other peninsular species of Lanius are as follows :

1. *L. lahtora* Sykes, *L. excubitor var C.* Lath., Doodeea latora, Hind. This large Shrike is an inhabitant of open low jungles throughout the country, and towards the more northern parts of the peninsula is found frequenting bushes and low trees in the open plains. It never approaches villages, and is a shy, wary bird and difficult of approach, and perhaps is the least numerous of any of the species.

2. *L. Erythronotus,* Vigors. Rufous backed Shrike. This, though occasionally found in the more wooded parts of the country in the Carnatic is only at all common in the neighbourhood of the jungles of the west coast, and is very abundant on the top of the Neilgherries.

3. *L. Hardwickii* Vigors. Bay backed Shrike of Latham. This enters gardens and is the most generally spread of all the Indian Shrikes.

4. *L. cristatus* L. after Edwards pl. 74.. *L. rutilus* var. A., and *L. superciliosus* var. A. of Latham ; *L. melanotis* Valenc : perhaps also white cheeked S. of Latham, and *L. phœnicurus* of Pallas (apud Latham.) This species, only lately accurately defined, escaped my notice when writing the Catalogue of Birds of Southern India, having overlooked it as the young of L. Hardwickii. It is found chiefly about hedge rows, and detached trees in the more cultivated parts of the country, and I am inclined to believe is migratory in the South of India.

The *L. tephronotus* of Vigors, grey backed Strike of Latham, *L. nipalensis* of Hodgson, is not found in the South of India.

XVIII

Palæornis columboides,

Printed by Litho O.V. Histnarujo

ORD. INSESSORES.

TRIBE SCANSORES.

FAM. PSITTACIDÆ.

GEN. PALÆORNIS.

PLATE XVIII.

PALÆORNIS COLUMBOIDES *Vigors.*

BLUE WINGED PARROQUET.

Synon.—*P. melanorhyncha* Sykes, (the female,) Jerdon Cat. No. 203.

This elegantly coloured Parroquet belongs to the division long ago characterised by Vigors, which seems peculiar to the Asiatic province, more especially to the continent of India, and which is, with the exception of *Psittaculus*, the only form of this family known in India, and comprises several well marked species. Previously to obtaining this bird, I had heard from several sportsmen of a blue parroquet said to be common in the depths of the forests of Malabar. I first procured it at Trichoor, and afterwards in various other localities on the West coast, and on the sides of the Neilgherries up to a height of 5000 feet. As Colonel Sykes has it in his Catalogue, it probably extends along the range of western ghauts for some distance, but I have not heard of its having been procured in any other locality.

It keeps entirely to the depths of the forests, and frequents only the loftiest trees. Its flight is very rapid aud elegant, and it associates in small flocks. Its cry, though similar in character to the harsh call of the common Parroquet, is much more mellow, subdued, and agreeable. I have only once seen this bird in captivity; it would however be a very desirable addition to our aviaries.

I have not seen the description of *P. Columboides* by Vigors, which is in the Zoological Journal, but from Sykes' comparative description of his *melanorhyncha*, I have no doubt that ours is that species, Sykes' bird being the female, which appears always to retain the black bill, and Mr. Blyth informs me that the adult female of *P. ponticerianus* also has the beak black.

The Hindustani name *Muddengour Totah,* was applied to a specimen of this bird by one Shikaree, but in Latham's work I see that the *P. ponticerianus* is known by that name, and I presume it was incorrectly applied in my case, as the *columboides* is a species of such comparative local distribution.

Description. Male. Plumage generally of a light dove colour ; a black collar extends round the neck, widest beneath and reaching to the base of the lower mandible, and bordered posteriorly by a light bluish green collar ; face pale green ; lower part of back, rump and upper tail coverts also light green ; wing coverts dark green edged with yellowish white ; shoulders blackish green ; lower part of abdomen and under tail coverts very pale yellow green ; quills and centre tail feathers blue, the latter tipped with yellowish white ; the rest of the tail feathers green on the outer side, yellow on the inner side of the shaft, those next the centre feathers almost blue on the outer side. Bill coral red above, dusky beneath. Irides pale yellow, Legs and feet plumbeous. Length 15 to 16 inches, Wing 5¾ to 6, Tail 8½ to 9.

The Female differs in having a dusky black bill, and in the plumage generally being more tinged with green.

The other Indian species of Palæornis are, 1st *P. Alexandri,* Raee Totah H. Rare in Southern India—Common in Ceylon—I obtained a specimen in Travancore which was struck by a Shaheen *(Falco Shaheen)* and was dropped on my firing at it. I also found it breeding in the hole of a large tree in the north of the Deccan. 2d *P. Torquatus,* Lyber Totah H. Abundant over all India, feeding not only on fruit, but also very destructive to grain. 3d *P. cyanocephalus* L., *P. bengalensis, erythrocephalus,* and *gingianus* Auct. Tooeeah Totah H. An inhabitant of all the jungly districts of India, and also found about well wooded towns. It visits the open country in large flocks from July to September. Other species found in the Himalayas are *P. schistaceus,* Hodgson, and *P. ponticerianus* Auct.

XIX

Malacocircus griseus.

Printed by Litho. [illegible]

ORD. INSESSORES.

FAM. CRATEROPODINÆ.

GEN. MALACOCIRCUS.

PLATE XIX.

MALACOCIRCUS GRISEUS.

WHITE HEADED BABBLER.

Synon.—*Turdus griseus* Latham. *Thimalia grisea* Jerdon Cat. No. 92.

Among the many birds peculiar to this vast continent, there are none, in my opinion, so peculiarly characteristic of it, as that genus of which the species here figured, is by no means an inconspicuous member. The Mynas, it is true, the Parroquets, and the Drongo Shrikes, are spread over the same extent at least, but none of these exclusively inhabit India, as these birds are at present believed to do. I have often amused myself in imagining that they are not inapt representatives of the Hindoos; certainly as far as their frequent congregating together, and their incessant noisy chattering and gabbling, they agree; and were I disposed to carry on the similitude further, it would not I think be a difficult task. It is not a little remarkable too that in Southern India there are several kinds which in some measure correspond in geographical distribution with the principal Hindoo races of this part of the country. We have the *M. Malcolmi* in the country of the Mahrattas; the subject of the present plate nearly confined to, and at all events most abundant in the Carnatic, the country of the Tamools; a very closely allied species inhabits Travancore and Cochin, the province of the Malyalum race; it is probable that a fourth species is to be found in the Canarese districts; one or perhaps two species dwell in the forests bordering the western ghauts; another prefers the eastern ghauts, and jungles of the northern circars, among the Gentoos; Ceylon possesses a distinct kind; Bengal has at least one or two more; and the elevated forests of the Wynaad, and the edges of the higher mountains of the Western ghauts, are the habitat of a very distinct species, somewhat allied in colouring to the *Crateropi*, which curiously enough at a higher level inhabit the same regions, to the exclusion of the *Malacocirci*, though in very limited number, whilst in the North of India species of the former genus abound, and descend I believe, nearly to the plains.

The genus *Malacocircus* was first defined by Swainson, in his Zoological Illustrations, and was founded on a species from Ceylon. It is distinguished by its high and compressed bill, gradually arching from the base, soft bowed wings, large broad and soft tail, strong legs and feet, light coloured irides, usually white or pale yellow, and sombre and uninviting plumage.

The white headed Babbler is found throughout the Carnatic, extending on the one side into the Northern Circars, and on the West into the neighbouring portions of the table land, to a greater or less distance. It is extremely common and abundant in the Carnatic, and is to be found in every hedge, avenue, and garden. Like the others of its genus it always associates in families of six, seven, eight or more; even in the breeding season the parent birds feeding in company with their former companions. One may be seen suddenly dropping to the ground from some tree, and is followed in succession, though perhaps not immediately, by each of the flock. They hop about, turning over fallen leaves, and examining all the herbage around the base of trees, a very favorite spot, or on a hedge side, never venturing to any distance from cover, being aware of their tardy powers of flight. They are occasionally seen seeking insects or grain, from heaps of dung, whence they have received their common denomination as well from the French, (Fouille-merde,) as from the English, (Dirt bird,) who are on this account prejudiced against them. They generally feed at some little distance apart from each other, but now and then if a richer prize than usual is spied out, two or more will meet and struggle for it; and now and then, one of them will make a clumsy flight after a grasshopper, seeking safety by its wings, and not unfrequently eluding its awkward pursuer. On being driven from the ground, or leaving it from choice, their hunger being satisfied, they fly up to the nearest tree, hopping and climbing up the larger branches, and if you happen to be watching them they do not stop till they have reached the top, or the opposite side whence they fly off in single and extended file as before. They often appear to pick insects off the branches of trees. They are familiar, if undisturbed, feeding often close to houses, but if watched or followed, they become circumspect, disperse, and hide themselves. Their cry is a loud sibilous or whispering sort of chatter, which they repeat all at once, sometimes when feeding, or when any unusual sight attracts their attention, and often without any apparent object at all. They have no song. Their flight is slow and laborious, performed by a few rapid strokes of the wings alternating with a sailing with outspread pinions. I have often found the nest of this bird, which is composed of small twigs and roots carelessely and loosely put together, in general at no great height from the ground ; it lays three or four blue eggs. I have found them breeding at all times from January to July, and even later, but do not know if they ever have two broods in the year. The black and white crested Cuckoo, *(oxylophus edolius)* appears to select this bird to act as foster parent to her own progeny, and she lays a greenish blue egg. They are readily caught by a spring trap baited with grain, with one of their kind put in the centre as a lure. The Shikra or Chipka, *(Accipiter badius)* is sometimes flown at them, and causes a a general consternation. After the first burst of alarm and gabbling, they cease their chattering, separate, and disperse, and do not, like the bolder Mahratta Babbler, (M. malcolmi) come to the rescue of their unfortunte companion. This latter species often mobs the Shikra.

The white headed Babbler is called *Keyr* in Hindustani, *Cheenda* or *Seeda* in Teloogoo, in Tamool '*Kullee Kooravee*' or 'hedge bird,' and in Malyalum the allied species is called '*Kooleyan*.'

I add a brief description. General shade of plumage light brownish grey, head and nape yellowish white, more marked in some than in others,—feathers of the back dark, lightest on the shaft and the edges, rump feathers pale fawn, feathers of the chin and throat dark in the centre, with the base and extremity blueish white, forming a band very distinct from the surrounding plumage. Breast, abdomen, and under tail coverts pale yellowish fawn colour. Most of the feathers especially the back and rump, are much decomposed, and are blueish white at their base. Quills and tail brown obsoletely barred with darker bands, central tail feathers light at their base. Length 9 to $9\frac{1}{2}$ inches, Wing $4\frac{2}{10}$, Tail $4\frac{1}{4}$, Tarsus $1\frac{3}{10}$, Hind toe and claw $\frac{7}{10}$ths. Bill (at front) $\frac{7}{10}$th. at gape about $\frac{9}{10}$ths. Irides pale yellow white. Bill and legs pale yellowish with a tinge of flesh color.

The other species of Malacocircus found in the peninsula are as follows 1st *M.*

affinis, new species. This is the one before alluded to, as being very closely allied to *griseus*. It differs most remarkably in the form of the bill, which is shorter, higher at the base, and if any thing more compressed. With regard to coloration it is very similar indeed to the Carnatic one. The white on the head is perhaps less pure, and the band on the throat less dark, but these are the chief points of difference. The feet and claws are however somewhat larger in this, more especially the hind foot and claw, which is about one tenth of an inch longer than griseus. Length 9 to $9\frac{1}{3}$, Wing $4\frac{1}{10}$, Tail $4\frac{1}{4}$, Tarsus $1\frac{3}{10}$, Hind toe and claw $\frac{8}{10}$ths, Bill at front hardly $\frac{6}{10}$, at gape 8 $\frac{1/2}{10}$ths, height at base nearly $\frac{3}{10}$.

I have at present two specimens of this bird from Travancore, but they agree with each other very closely in the form of the bill and in the structure of the legs, the most essential points of difference from *griseus*.

This may be the same as the Canarese variety which I long ago pointed out from Mr. Elliot's M. S. S. notes as being probably distinct from *griseus*, but there are certain points of difference in the description, and it is possible that this may constitute another species. Mr. Elliot describes the species as follows. Plumage above, chin, and throat brown cinereous, shaft of the feathers lighter; head and nape whitish; rump cinereous; tail brown with indistinct darker bars; belly whitish like the head. Irides silver white, Bill and legs white, Length $9\frac{1}{4}$ inches. Should it prove distinct I would propose the name of *Elliotti*.

2nd *M. Malcomi*, *Thimalia Malcomi* Sykes, Jerdon Cat. No. 90. *Garrulus albifrons*, Gray and Hardwicke. On my pointing out to Mr. Blyth that the figure under the above name in Gray and Hardwicke was probably that of a *Malacocircus*, that gentleman at once agreed with me, and moreover pointed out its probable identity with *M. Malcomi* of which I had sent him specimens. It is possible however that the drawing may represent an allied species of Northern India.* This large babbler is found, though rarely and only in jungles, in the Carnatic, and here chiefly towards the range of Eastern ghauts; I saw it at Coonoor on the Neilgherries, and M. Delessert showed me specimens from the Shervaroy hills near Salem, but its chief metropolis is the North western portion of the Deccan or Table land, including the Southern Mahratta country, the Deccan of Sykes, and generally

* I may here remark that the late excellent rules for Nomenclature drawn up by Gray Strickland and others do not provide for a case like the present, viz. whether the name attached to a published *figure* hold precedence or otherwise, of a name attached to a published *description*. On this point depends the correct specific name of many of the birds figured in Gray and Hardwicke, and I beg to draw the attention of the above named Zoologists to it.

the Mahratta portion of the Nizam's dominions, not extending further than the boundaries of the trap formation, which curiously enough divides the Mahratta and the Telinga races, the latter commencing nearly with the granite formation which extends through the eastern part of the Nizam's dominions. In all the district mentioned above the *M. Malcolmi* is as common as the *M. griseus* is in the Carnatic, being found near every village, and in every clump of trees. It is much more noisy than its congeners, and flies generally in larger flocks, twelve and fifteen being a common number. I have found the nest and eggs which closely resemble those of *griseus.* It is called *Ghoghoye* in Hindustani, *Gowa Seeda* in Teloogoo, and sometimes *Verree cheenda,* or mad Babbler.

3rd *M. Somervillei, Thimalia Somervillei,* Sykes P. Z. S. 1832, not of Jerdon Cat. No. 91. Thus described by Colonel Sykes. Reddish brown; abdomen, vent, lower back and tail, light rufous, the latter obsoletely banded with darker; quills brown; the feathers of the throat and breast marked in the middle with blueish, Bill and feet yellow. Length $9\frac{1}{5}$ Tail $4\frac{1}{2}$, Irides bright yellow. Found in the ghauts only (viz: in the more Northern portion about N. L. 17° to 20°).

4th. *M. malabaricus* new species? *M. Somervillei* Jerdon Cat. No. 91. Now that I am better acquainted with the birds of this genus, and know how closely they approximate, I have little hesitation in separating the bird which I formerly referred to *Somervillei.* It differs from that species, as described by Sykes, in having the back of a cinereous brown instead of a reddish brown, and in the lower part of the back and tail not being rufous. In this respect Sykes' bird approaches somewhat to *M. Earlei* of Blyth, the only one I have seen with a rufous tail. Should however the description of *Somervillei* be faulty, mine may yet prove to be identical with it, as they both inhabit the western ghauts, though in different latitudes. My species is found in the forests of Malabar, and on the sides of the Neilgherries up to the very edge of the hills. I add its dimentions. Length $9\frac{1}{4}$ or so Wing $4\frac{1}{10}$th. Tail $4\frac{1}{2}$. Tarsus $1\frac{4}{10}$ths. Hind toe and claw $\frac{8}{10}$ths. Bill (at front) nearly $\frac{8}{10}$ths. at gape 1 inch.

5. *M. orientalis,* new species? Another species referred by me to the *Somervillei* of my Catalogue is found in the jungles of the Carnatic, and more especially among those of the Eastern ghauts, where it is very abundant, whence the name I have proposed. It differs from the last, *malabaricus,* in the prevalent lighter tint of the plumage, especially beneath, where it is almost white, contrasting strongly with the rufous tint of the other

the tail feathers too are not so wide as in *malabaricus,* a similar difference existing, I find on comparing specimens, between *griseus* of the East coast and *affinis* of the West, which I had not previously observed. This bird is the *Pedda* or *Adavee Seeda* of the Telingas. I add its dimensions. Length $9\frac{1}{4}$. Wing $4\frac{1}{10}$. Tail $4\frac{1}{4}$. Tarsus hardly $1\frac{4}{10}$. Hind toe and claw $\frac{8}{10}$ Bill (at front) $7\frac{\frac{1}{2}}{10}$ths. at gape about 1. I may state that I haave obtained many specimens of this species all agreeing exactly in colour.

6th. *M. terricolor* Hodgson. Mr. Blyth some time ago informed me that he had obtained this common Bengal species from Goomsoor, and I have now before me a specimen from that locality in Lord Arthur Hay's collection. I obtained a specimen of this species when in Goomsoor some years ago, and referred to it in my Catalogue, under *Somervillei,* as probably distinct, though the form of the bill mentioned there appears to have been accidental. On comparing it with some specimens sent me by Mr. Blyth from Calcutta there appear some differences; it is somewhat smaller in all its dimentions, more uniform in its colour above, and more rufous beneath, but it is otherwise so very closely allied that I shall not at present separate it, but should it hereafter prove to be distinct I would propose the name of *Orissæ* from the name of the district. I add its dimensions. Length 9, Wing 4, Tail 4, Tarsus $1\frac{4}{10}$, Hind toe andclaw $\frac{8}{10}$ths, Bill, at front $\frac{7}{10}$ths. at gape $1\frac{\frac{1}{2}}{10}$th.

A Calcutta specimen measures about $9\frac{1}{2}$ inches or more Wing $4\frac{2}{10}$, Tail $4\frac{1}{4}$. Tars $1\frac{5}{10}$. Bill at front $\frac{8}{10}$ths, at gape $1\frac{1}{10}$th, higher than in the Goomsoor specimen. This species is is the *Turdus Canorus* of Linnæus from Edward's figure of his Brown Indian Thrush, but Mr. Blyth rejects the name 'from its extreme inappropriateness, the bird having a most particularly harsh voice (atch, atch) and no pretensions whatever to be musical, in the least degree. It is probably the M. *striatus* of a catalogue of Bengal birds in the Ann. and Mag. Nat. Hist. 1843.' It is the *Chatarrhæa* and *Sath Bhaee* (seven Brothers,) of the Bengalese. It extends into Nepal and Assam.

7th. *M. subrufus. Thimalia subrufa,* Jerdon Catal. No. 93. *T. pœcilorhyncha* De la Fresnaye, Rev. Zool. de la Soc. Cuv. 1840. This is a very distinct species from all the previous ones, allied in coloring to the *Crateropi.* It frequents bamboo jungles in the elevated region of Wynaad, and along the edges of the Western Ghauts. I observed it once at Coonoor on the edge of the Neilgherry hills.

Besides the species enumerated above we have the *M. striatus* Swainson from Ceylon. A Cingalese specimen which (Mr. Blyth remarks) corresponded closely with

Swainson's figure, much resembles my *malabaricus*, but differs in the paler and more cinereous hue of the feathers of the head and back, in the rufous of the lower parts being more uniform, in wanting the pale longitudinal central markings of the feathers of the back and breast, and in the very distinct striation of the tertiaries and tail. 'Length 9½, Tail 4¼, Tarsus 1⅛, Bill to gape 1 inch' (Blyth.) It was founded on a Ceylon species which Mr. Swainson identified with a bird in the Paris Museum labelled *Gracula striata*. It is, *Cossyphus striatus* of Dumeril (Blyth), and *Philanthus striatus* of Lesson.

It is not impossible however that the *striatus* of the French museum is one of the allied species, either *terricolor, malabaricus,* or *orientalis,* which Swainson might have readily enough mistaken for it. Lesson says it was from Bengal; if so it is probably *terricolor*. Mr. Strickland in his notice of Gray's Genera of Birds says 'the earliest synonym of *malac. striatus* is *Turdus griseus*' but that this is erroneous there can be little doubt after what has been stated above, though it is a mistake which might easily have occurred to any one.

Another species, *M. Earlei,* has been described by Mr. Blyth J. A. S. 1844 p. 369. Its colouring allies it something to *M. Somervillei* Sykes, but in form it more resembles *malcolmi* or *Thimalia chatarhæa* of Franklin. It is found in heavy reed and grass jungle in Bengal, and extends also to Nepal, but I have not yet procured it in Southern India.

Other species probably will be found in the North of India; *M. Somervillei* is said in Royle's list to be found as far North as the plains near Saharunpore, but it is probably distinct.

A somewhat aberrant species, intermediate to *malacocircus* and *megalurus* exists in the *Thìmalia chatarhæa* of Franklin, Jerdon Cat. No 94. It is the *Gracula caudata* of the Paris museum, *Thimalia caudata* De la Fresnaye, *megalurus caudatus* Lesson, *cossyphus caudatus* Dumeril, and *megalurus isabellinus* of Swainson. It certainly differs somewhat in form from the typical *malacocirci,* as well from the true *megaluri.* It perhaps resembles the former more in its habits, frequenting low bushy jungle in large flocks, and the latter in the tone of its plumage, and dark irides. Its note is a pleasing sort of low whistle. It has an extensive distribution, having been sent to the Calcutta museum from Scinde It is called *Doomree* in Hindustani from its long tail. Mr. Blyth remarks that the little *Thimalia hyperythra* Franklin, Jerdon Cat. No. 96, is 'so closely allied to *Malac. subrufus* that I almost think it should be ranged with it.' It is the *Shah Doomree* in Hindustani, and *Pundee jitta* or Pig bird in Teloogoo, a name given from its habit of making its way under the bushes, never shewing itself above.

The *Thimalia hypoleuca* of Franklin, *T. Horsfieldii*, Jard. and Selby, Jerd. Cat. No. 95, has been separated by Mr. Hodgson under the name of *Chrysomma*. Its name in Hindustani is *Goolal chusm*, or *Red eye*, from the orange orbits, whence also Hodgson's name. I see it is described in Latham as Var. A. of the Red-eyed Bunting (*Emberiza Calfat.*)

In my Catalogue of Birds published in the Madras Journal of Literature and Science 1839, I remarked as follows under *Thimalia Somervillei*. "From the peculiar distribution of this truly Indian genus and the general similarity of colour, I am inclined to think that hereafter other species may be separated, closely allied in plumage and general structure, yet differing in some permanent character both of structure and plumage, as well as in geographical distribution." The present article shows that this has in a great measure been verified, though not so completely as I could have wished, owing as well to a want of specimens, as to want of observation of the species in its native haunts, and more especially its notes, which differ considerably in all those I have myself observed. I hope however before this work is brought to a conclusion, to have ascertained more precisely the distinctness of some of the species here indicated, and shall mention the result in an appendix, in which all errors of nomenclature, or additional information will be inserted. I am satisfied that most of them will hold to be good species, as it is well known that in many genera the species approximate so very closely as to be distinguished with difficulty.

XX

Petrocincla manillensis.

Printed by Litho C.V. Kistnarajoo.

ORD. INSESSORES.

FAM. MERULIDÆ.

GEN. PETROCINCLA.

PLATE XX.

PETROCINCLA PANDOO. *Sykes.*

INDIAN BLUE ROCK THRUSH.

Synon.—*P. Maal*—Sykes—(the female.)

I affixed the name of *Petrocincla Manillensis* to the drawing of this bird, as Mr. Blyth had suggested to me the probability of its being that species, with which I agreed at once, the more readily that in Lesson's Traité *P. Manillensis* is mentioned as from India. Mr. Blyth however subsequently obtained the real *Manillensis* from Luçonia, and found that our present is a distinct tho' very closely allied species, and accordingly Sykes' name will stand good. A third allied species, from Tenasserim and Darjeeling, Mr. Blyth has designated *P. affinis*. Swainson's excellent name *Petrocincla* will have to give way to *Monticola.*

The Indian blue rock thrush is extended over most of the continent of India, and has most probably a still more extended geographical distribution, as it is migratory here, retiring to the north to breed at the approach of the hot weather. Towards the south of the peninsula it is very rare. I have only seen it at all common on the Neilgherries—and now and then a single stray specimen on some rocky and jungly hill in the Carnatic. In the Deccan however it becomes more abundant, and there, chiefly, almost exclusively frequents the old walls and remains of forts so common there, every village however small being surrounded by a high mud wall. On two or three occasions I observed it in Cantonment on the top of a stable or out-building. Mr. Elliot in his M.S.S. notes on Indian Birds, from which I drew much information in the compilation of my Catalogue of Indian Birds, mentions that he found this bird numerous on the coast from Vingorla to Cambay, frequenting the neighbourhood of villages and houses, and even so tame as to enter verandahs. It is in general a very shy and wary bird, usually concealing itself on some rock or stone, perhaps just showing its head, and taking flight if approached. I have often in open ground followed it long in vain, its rapid and undulating flights becoming more extended as its suspicions become roused. It feeds on the ground on coleopterous insects chiefly.

Its name in Hindustani is *Shama,* and it is said to be sometimes caged by Faqueers and others for its song, which is highly prized in the north of India, but its musical qualities appear unknown in the south, and the *Copsychus macrourus* appears known as the Shama or Shahmour in Bengal.

Description. Male. Of a dusky blue tint throughout, many of the feathers dusky-tipped, Wings and tail dusky brown. Female, of a greyish brown tinge above, beneath paler, mottled with whiteish, and under tail coverts barred with dusky. Bill and legs black. Irides deep brown. Length $8\frac{1}{2}$ to 9 inches, Extent 14, Wing $4\frac{8}{10}$, Tail 3 to $3\frac{1}{2}$, Bill (at front) $\frac{8}{10}$ ths.—Tarsus $1\frac{1}{10}$ th.—Weighs nearly 2 ounces.

The *P. Manillensis* differs in the Male having the under parts from the breast, the axillaries, and under wing coverts, bright ferruginous, and in the female (*T. eremita* of Gmelin) being much paler beneath. The tail is perfectly squared. It is found in Luçonia and China, &c.

P. affinis Blyth differs from this last in having much less ferruginous, and in the shape of the tail, which has its outermost feathers nearly half an inch shorter than the middle ones.

In *P. Pandoo* the tail is intermediate in shape to these two.

Vinago bicincta,

Printed by Litho C.V. Hist.

ORD. RASORES.

FAM. COLUMBIDÆ.

GEN. VINAGO.

PLATE XXI.

VINAGO BICINCTA.

PURPLE AND ORANGE BREASTED GREEN PIGEON

Synon.—*V. vernans* var. Lesson. *V. bicincta* Jerdon, Catal. No. 289 and *V. unicolor* No. 289 bis.

The group of green pigeons has long been separated from the other pigeons by Cuvier and Vieillot, but I see that the name given by the latter author '*Treron*' has been adopted by Gray and others, having been first published, though Cuvier alleges that he first named many of these genera in the museum of the 'Jardin des plantes' but he did not publish them until the appearance of his 'Regne animal,' and that in the mean time Vieillot adopted the genera, and gave them names of his own. The group is a very natural one and contains a number of species, several from continental India, many from the Malay countries, and some from Africa. They are distinguished by their green plumage, thick soft bills, flat broad soles, the emarginate quills, and (the Indian species at least) by their blue and red coloured irides. Their habits are strictly arboreal, and they feed on fruit alone, never resorting to hard seeds like most of the family.

The species of which the accompanying is a drawing was first described by myself in the Madras Journal. Strickland I see doubted its distinctness from *V. vernans* of the Malay countries, but Mr. Blyth who has procured both fully recognises it as a distinct though closely allied species,and has sent me specimens of each for comparison. Our peninsular bird is a rare, and by no means abundant species. I have only seen it myself on two or three occasions, and always in the close vicinity of the sea; once in the Northern Circars,once in the

Carnatic, and once on the Malabar coast, but I have lately obtained specimens from Travancore, and also from the jungles of the Eastern ghauts inland from Nellore. Mr. Blyth too has obtained it at Calcutta from the Botanic garden there where it breeds, and also from the Sunderbunds, and has received it from Arracan, and other places to the Eastward. I observed it myself always in small flocks.

The note of the green pigeons is a very pleasing full toned rolling whistle. Though usually impatient of confinement they will sometimes live for a long time when caged, and properly attended to.

Description. Back of head and neck above blue grey; forehead, top of head, face, chin, throat and belly, yellow green ; the rest of the plumage above green ; a broad band of orange or bright cinnamon yellow on the breast, separated from the green of the throat by a light purple band; lower part of abdomen and vent yellow, some of the feathers streaked with green; under tail coverts entirely cinnamon colour; tail above grey with a central dark band, and edged lighter, beneath almost black, with a broad whitish margin; edges of the greater wing coverts broadly margined with yellow.

Length about 10½ inches, wing 6, Tail 4¼. Bill glaucous white, legs lake red. Irides smalt blue with an exterior circle of carmine.

The young (or it may be the female) differs from the adult male in wanting entirely the purple and orange bands on the breast, and in the under tail coverts being mixed with white.

The Malayan *V. vernans,* of which a specimen is now before me, differs in having whole head, face and throat grey, in the purple band being much wider and extending round the neck, in the deeper tint of the orange, in the upper tail coverts being tawny and in the tail wanting the broad edging of white beneath &c. &c. It is also a smaller bird. I add the dimensions. Length about 9½, wing 5½, tail 4.

The other species of green pigeon found in the South of India are as follows.

1st *V. chlorigaster* Blyth, *V. Jerdoni* Strickland, *V. militaris,* Jerdon Catalogue No. 286. This has only been recently recorded as distinct from the true *militaris* of Northern India.

2nd. *V. malabarica* Jerdon n. s., *V. aromatica* Jerdon Cat. No. 287, and 288 (the female). On sending a specimen of this bird to Mr. Blyth, that gentleman informed me that it differs from the true *aromaticus* of Northern India in the form of the bill and in some other particulars. I have therefore given it provisionally the name of *malabarica* from its habitat, which is chiefly the forests of Malabar, and the other high jungles of the western coast. I add what Mr. Blyth says on their points of difference. "The two species agree exactly in size and colouring of feathers, except that yours has a yellow throat in both sexes; bu the form of the bill is essentially different, and there are several other distinctions. *Tr. aromaticus* verus (from Bengal and Arracan) has a very much stronger bill, the corneous portion of which reaches back to tbe frontal feathers; its colour is glaucous green with the soft and tumid portion at the sides of the upper mandible vermilion, forming a large and conspicuous spot; in your species the basal half of the bill is soft and tumid; *aromaticus* has the eye surrounded by a naked space of a livid blue, in yours the space surrounding the eyes is feathered to the orbit; lastly *aromaticus* has the legs and toes very bright vermilion contrasting forcibly with the red of those of *bicinctus*, whereas those of your species are described as 'lake.'

XXII

R.E.B. lith

Fred. lith. Linn. imp.

PASTOR BLYTHII

ORD. INSESSORES.

TRIBE CONIROSTRES.

FAM. STURNIDÆ.

GEN. PASTOR.

PLATE XXII.

PASTOR BLYTHII. Jerdon.

WHITE HEADED MYNA.

Synon.—*P. Malabaricus* Jerdon, Catal. No. 166.

The White headed Myna figured here was considered by me in my Catalogue to be the *Malabaricus* of Authors, which Wagler had erroneously identified with the female of *P. Pagodarum,* but Mr. Blyth some time ago suggested to me that the name *Malabaricus* more properly belonged to the grey-headed species found over all the continent of India, and which I had alluded to in my Catalogue as being probably distinct from the white-headed one. Mr. Strickland I see confirms this, and has suggested my naming this anew. I have therefore given it the specific appellation of *Blythii* after the present talented and indefatigable Curator of the Museum of the Asiatic Society of Calcutta.

This bird belongs to the small division of Mynas for which Lesson has proposed the name *Sturnia,* and which is typified by the *P. Pagodarum.* Their make is smaller and lighter than that of the Common Mynas, and their habits in general perhaps are more arboreal. Mr. Blyth remarks that they are seldom seen on the ground, but this statement must be qualified with regard to *P. Pagodarum* which feeds chiefly on the ground, and often among cattle like the Common Myna, although, as I long ago remarked in my Catalogue, when I did observe this bird in the Northern part of the Peninsula, it was only on trees.

The white-headed Myna is only found in the forests of Malabar and the more Southern portions of the West Coast, and here it is by no means either common or abundant. It frequents lofty trees on which it procures its food, consisting of insects and their larvæ, and small shells (Bulimi) which I have found entire in its stomach. Its usual cry is neither so loud nor so harsh as that of most of the Mynas, and it has a very pleasing song. I dare say, like the others of it genus, it nidificates in holes of trees, and lays 3 or 4 greenish blue eggs, but I have not had an opportunity of observing this.

Description. Whole head, neck, throat and breast, beautiful silky white ; back and wing coverts grey ; quills dusky black ; abdomen, sides, and under tail coverts, rufous ; centre tail feathers grey, tipped with rufous and dark shafted, the intermediate ones grey on the outer web, rufous at the tip, and black internally, the rufous increasing as far as the outer tail feathers, which are entirely rufous, except at the base. Bill blue at the base, greenish in the centre, and yellow at the tip. Irides blueish white—legs and feet reddish yellow, claws pale yellow—Length 8 to $8\frac{1}{2}$ inches—Wing $4\frac{2}{10}$—Tail $2\frac{8}{10}$ to 3 inches—Bill (at front) nearly $\frac{8}{10}$ ths.—Tarsus 1 inch.

It differs from the common grey-headed Myna in being larger in all its dimensions, in the colour of the head and neck, in the primaries not being tipped with grey, and in some other slight points. This last species, *Malabaricus* verus, occurs here only in the cold weather I find, and is generally dispersed through the Southern part of the Peninsula, preferring of course the more wooded portions of the country.

XXIII

Dendrocygna major

Printed by Litho. C.V. Kistnarajo

ORD. NATATORES.

FAM. ANATIDÆ.

GEN. DENDROCYGNA.

PLATE XXIII.

DENDROCYGNA MAJOR.

LARGE WHISTLING TEAL.

Among the many species of Duck found in this country during the cold weather there are but few peculiar to it, the great majority being birds of extended geographical distribution, and ranging from the torrid regions to the limits of the Arctic circle. The genus *Dendrocygna* however appears to be peculiar to India and its isles, and contains several species, very closely allied indeed, but yet sufficiently characterized as distinct forms. Horsfield indicates other species besides his *Javanica,* but merely calls them varieties, although the natives, he tells us, distinguish them by separate names. Colonel Sykes has characterized the common species of this country apart from Horsfield's under the name of '*awsuree*,' and in my Catalogue of Indian birds I described the present species under the name of *D. major*. It appears contrary to my first supposition to be more generally spread than I had imagined, for I obtained specimens occasionally at Nellore, and Mr. Blyth has procured it at Calcutta where it appears not rare, though not nearly so common or abundant as the smaller species. At Jaulnah in the North of the Deccan it was as common as *awsuree*. I have no information of its occurrence out of the peninsula of India, but it is probable enough that it may be one of the Javanese varieties of Horsfield.

The *Dendrocygnæ* are called Whistling Teal by sportsmen in India from the sibilous cry they have, and their Hindustani name of '*Sillee*' also signifies whistler. They are found in flocks of various size, frequenting chiefly the smaller and more reedy and grassy tanks. Their flight is more heavy than that of the generality of the duck tribe, and they can be readily distinguished at a distance even by the comparatively lazy flapping of their wings. They breed in the hot weather, laying several eggs of a dirty white colour, spotted all over with rusty red: these are said to be laid in a tuft of grass, but I have not myself found them in situ.

The flesh of the Whistling Teal is in general poor, tough, and fishy, and they are not therefore held in any esteem for the table, though at times I believe they are more palateable, especially after being kept in a Tealery for some time.

I add a description of the large Whistling Teal.

Head and neck chesnut, darker on the top of the head, whence a dark line extends down the back of the neck; chin, throat and fore neck very pale; on the centre of the neck there is a broad patch of small whitish somewhat hackled feathers. Upper part of the back and scapulars deep brown, the feathers edged with chesnut, lower part of the back black, lesser wing coverts dark marroon, other wing coverts, wings and tail dusky black—beneath chesnut, under tail coverts and a few of the upper ones yellowish white, the feathers on the sides of the body elongated, chesnut on one side of the shaft, and yellowish white edged with dark brown on the other. Bill and legs plumbeous Irides dark brown. Length 20 to 21 inches—Wing 9¼, Tail 2¼, Tarsus 2, middle toe with claw 3½, Bill at front $1\frac{8}{10}$ at gape 2¼.

This duck appears to me to bear a greater resemblance in colouring to Horsfield's species *Javanica* vel *arcuata* than the common one or *awsuree*, but it differs in size, in wanting the lunules of the breast and neck, in the small extent of the marroon colour on the wings, and in this being of a much duller hue; in the thigh feathers not being bordered with brown; and in the presence of the band of small whitish feathers on the neck, and in a few other minor points—Sykes' species differs from Horsfield's in its apparently smaller size, in wanting the lunules on back of neck and breast, and more particularly in its upper tail coverts being of the same marroon hue as the wing coverts, besides in several other particulars, and I have no doubt that it is a good and authentic species, although I see some Systematists have lately joined them. It is not improbably the smaller variety indicated by Horsfield to which the Javanese give the name of *Meliwis batu*, *Meliwis* being the common name of *Javanica*, and my D. *major* may also be the *Meliwis kembung* alluded to as another variety. The name of *Javanica* must stand for Horsfield's species, it having been first described under that name, that of *arcuata* having been subsequently given as the name by which Cuvier had distinguished it in the museum of Paris.

XXIV

Caprimulgus Indicus.

Printed by Litho. C.V. Kistnaraye.

ORD. INSESSORES.

TRIBE FISSIROSTRES

FAM. CAPRIMULGIDÆ.

GEN. CAPRIMULGUS.

PLATE XXIV.

CAPRIMULGUS INDICUS.

LARGE INDIAN NIGHTJAR.

Synon.—*Capr. Indicus* Lath. Jerdon (Cat. No. 251.)

The vague and imperfect description by Latham of his *C. Indicus* without any measurements could scarcely have led to the identification of the subject of our present plate had it not been for the figure in Gray and Hardwicke's 'Illustrations of Indian Zoology,' by which I was led in my Catalogue to refer my bird to that species; and as Latham elsewhere describes most of the other Indian Caprimulgi, Gray was probably justified in refering Hardwicke's figure to Latham's *Indicus*. The drawing however in Gray and Hardwicke represents a female, and the male has not that I know been previously figured.

This fine Nightjar has been found dispersed, though sparingly, over all India, and has even a still more extended geographical distribution, as Mr. Blyth has procured specimens from the East of Bengal, and even I believe from China. I procured my first specimens from the Neilgherries, but have since obtained some from other parts of the country, from the Deccan, the west coast, and even the Carnatic, but it is by no means a common species. It affects chiefly the more wooded portions of the country, being usually found, and more common in forests than in the open country, and here frequenting only shady gardens and large groves. On the Neilgherries it remains during the day in the dense woods there, issuing from them about sunset, and then coming into the open ground, and perching on stones and trees, and from thence pursuing its insect prey. It is now and then flushed from the woods when beating for woodcock, or other game, and more than one have fallen beneath the gun of the inexperienced sportsman, its extent of wing and lazy flapping having caused it to be mistaken for the woodcock. Its flight is at times very rapid and noiseless, performed with but few vibrations of its wings. When roused in the day time it flies (like others of the genus) but a short distance, and then suddenly alights, and squats close to the ground, never that I know perching in the day time; when hunting it often alights on a branch, usually sitting in the direction of the branch, and not across it, its feet being not adopted for grasping firmly.

The note of this Nightjar though somewhat like the sound of a stone scudding over Ice has not such a close resemblence to it as that of the common species (C. Asiaticus); it sounds some thing like Tew-yo-yo frequently repeated. Its chief food is moths and beetles.

The name *Nyctichelidon* or Night Swallow was sometime ago proposed to be substituted for Caprimulgus, and is a very good name, expressive at once of its habits and affinities, but as the Linnœan name cannot now propagate any error, it has not been considered necessary to change it. The Hindustani name for this genus is *Chippuk;* sometimes it is called popularly *Dub-chooree,* or *Dubhuk-chooree;* also *Andhe-chooree,* which names are given from its habit of close squatting before alluded to, the one meaning squat bird, and the other blind bird. Its common name in Teloogoo is '*Kuppa pitta*' or Frog bird, given however more from the actual resemblance of the flat head and large eyes and mouth, than as in France the name 'Crapaud volant' from a similarity in the call. The best Telinga shikarees however call this bird *As kappri gadoo,* a name, the meaning of which I have been unable to ascertain.

Mr. Blyth some time ago sent me a specimen corresponding very closely in plumage, but larger in all its proportions than my Neilgherry bird, which at first he was inclined to consider as distinct, but on re-examination, and comparison of many specimens from different part of the country he now considers as identical. My own specimens obtained from various localities differ much both in size and coloration, two specimens corresponding exactly being seldom met with. The male has always brighter plumage than the female, and appears at times to have the plumage darker and blacker than usual, but whether this is a seasonal variety, or one dependent on age I cannot now determine.

It is extremely difficult to describe accurately birds of the present mottled and varigated plumage, the more especially so when, as in the present instance, individual specimens vary so much. This however matters less when a tolerably faithful representation is given and accurate measurements are added. This species differs from the other Indian ones generally in the prevalent dark hue of the plumage—from *Asiaticus* and *Monticolus* it may be always distinguished at once by it feathered tarsi, and from *macrourus* by the dark wings and tail of the latter, and rufous breast &c. &c. I shall give no further description but add its measurements.

Total length from 10 to nearly 12 inches Wing 7 to 8½ Tail 5 to 5¾ Tarsus about $\frac{6}{10}$th.

The other Indian species of Caprimulgi are as follows:—1st *C. Asiaticus* Latham common Indian Nightjar—spread over all the peninsula, taking shelter under hedges, among bushes, in gardens, and feeding close to houses and even entering verandahs. I am still (as expressed in my Catalogue) inclined to believe that the species figured in Gray and Hardwicke as *Asiaticus* differs from the common species. I obtained what answered to this very closely in the North of the Deccan. It differs from the common one in its larger size, more prevalent and lighter grey tint of the plumage, and in some other trifling points, but I have now no specimens for comparrison. I at one time thought that it might be Sykes' *Mahrattensis* which otherwise I know not.*

2nd. *C. Monticolus* Franklin. When I compiled my Catalogue I had only met this Nightjar in Candeish, but I have since procured it in the neighbourhood of Madras, at Nellore, and other places. Mr. Blyth has also obtained it at Calcutta, so it appears tolerately generally distributed. I consider it to be the species described by Latham under *C. Indicus* from Sir J. Anstruther's drawings. It frequents chiefly rocky hills abounding with brushwood.

3rd. *C. macrourus* Horsf. I obtained specimens of this Nightjar from the range of Eastern Ghauts, and have seen a specimen from the Malabar coast in Lord Arthur Hay's collection. It is very closely allied to the species which Mr. Blyth had considered as *C. macrourus* of Horsfield, but is much smaller. Mr. Strickland however has compared the specimens in the India House museum from Java with Bengal specimens, and finds Horsfield's species much smaller, though very closely allied in plumage. The Calcutta bird will therefore stand as *C. gangeticus* Blyth, and Mr. B. naturally concludes that my species is the true *macrourus*. However in this genus where the plumage is so very similar it may still be a distinct species from the Javanese one, and if so I would propose the name of *atripennis*, and I add its di

* Mr. Blyth has just sent me for inspection a Nightjar sent by Hodgson as C. *innotatus*, which he considers as *Mahrattensis* It appears to me to be a very pale vanity of C. *Indicus* with much worn and a braded plumage.

mensions—Length about 11 inches, Wing about 7½, Tail 5½ to 6 inches. I consider it perhaps may be *C. Asiaticus var C.* Latham.

4th. *C. Mahrattensis* Sykes—I am inclined to consider from length of the tail as given by Sykes that this may turn out to be *C. Indicus.* I have a specimen from the West Coast smaller than the generality of individuals of this varying species. I may add that the probability of this conjecture is strengthened by Blyth having referred what I consider a mere variety of *C. Indicus* to Sykes' *Mahrattensis.*

XXV

Ceyx tridactyla,

Printed by Litho. C° Kistnawjoy

ORD. INSESSORES.

TRIBE FISSIROSTRES

FAM. HALCYONIDÆ. Sw.

GEN. CEYX.

PLATE XXV.

CEYX TRIDACTYLA.

PURPLE 3 TOED KINGFISHER.

Synon.—*A tridactyla,* L. Latham and Shaw (in part). *C. tridactyla,* Sykes Cat., not of Jardine and Selby. *A erithaca* var. (apud Shaw) and Red-headed Kingfisher, var. A. of Latham. *A purpurea,* Auct., Buffon P. E. 778.2, *Ceyx purpureus,* Lesson. *Ceyx microsoma* Burton P. Z. S., Jerdon Cat. No. 246.

The genus Ceyx was instituted by Lacepede for the 3 toed Kingfishers which form a small and beautiful group. The synonymy of the species however is involved in some obscurity, different names having been even recently applied to the same species by different authors. The description of the *A. tridactyla* of Linnæus (in Latham and Shaw) appears to correspond as nearly as possible with the bird figured here, but the name *tridactyla* has been applied by Jardine and Selby in their Illustrations of Ornithology pl. 55.2, to another species, which is decidedly the *A. Madagascariensis* of L., as described by Latham, and which is figured in the same plate of the Planches Enlumineés of Buffon as our present species. If Latham and Shaw are correct in their descriptions, and have faithfully followed Linnæus, there can I think be little doubt of the synonymy I have adopted, as I do not think it probable that Linnæus would have described the same bird under two different names; but if these authors have misplaced the original descriptions, then the rufous species will stand as *tridactyla,* with *Madagascariensis* as a synonym, and our bird will be *C. purpureus* (Gmel.), unless, Scopoli in the scientific names he has applied to the Birds described by Sonnerat should have given a prior name, and Sonnerat's bird prove identical with ours' as I suspect it will.

The purple 3 toed Kingfisher is a rare bird on the continent of India. I have obtained it in the Carnatic, and know that it has been found, though rarely, on the west coast, and in the Deccan. Mr. Blyth has not, that I am aware, obtained it from the vicinity of Calcutta, but has received specimens from Arracan where it appears not very uncommon, and thence it extends southward through the Malay peninsula, and many of the Isles.

I append a brief description.—Head and neck above of a rich sienna red, upper tail coverts and tail the same but, much dashed with shining lilac. A dark blue spot on forehead, and another of a brighter tinge over and behind the ears, this latter bordered beneath by a white mark. A stripe of beautiful glistening lilac from centre of eye above, extending over the blue spot. Back black, dashed with blue, wings black, coverts edged with dark blue, chin, throat and neck whitish, sides of head, and body beneath, rufous yellow. Bill and legs red.

Length 5 inches, Wing $2\frac{2}{10}$, Tail $1\frac{1}{10}$, Tars $\frac{3}{10}$, Bill (front) $1\frac{2}{10}$.

The other species of this group is the *Al. Madagascariensis* L., Rufous Kingfisher Latham No. 36., Javan Kingfisher Lath. No. 59., *A. purpurea var.* apud Shaw., Martin-pecheur roux de Madagascar, P. E. 778.1., *A. tridactyla,* Jard. and Selby Ill.Orn. pl. 55.2, and perhaps the *A. tridactyla* of Horsfield.

This is not found in the continent of India, but occurs in the south of the Malay peninsula, and thence extends eastward to the Isles.

The Kingfisher described by Sonnerat in his " voyage" pl. 32, as Le Martin-pecheur de l'isle de Luçon, the Luzonian K. of Latham No. 58, is perhaps the same as the subject of our present plate. If not, it will form a third and closely allied species.

The New Holland 3 toed Kingfishers have been separated from Ceyx by Swainson, under the name of *Alcyone.* Two species are described. 1st *A. azurea* (Lath.), *A. tribrachys,* Shaw, N. M., *Ceyx azureus,* Jard. and Sleby, Ill. Orn. 55. 1., *Ceyx cyana,* Lesson, *A australis,* Sw; and 2nd *C. Meningting* Lesson, Zool. de la Coquille, which would appear to be distinct from Horsfield's *A. Meningting,* and is certainly so, from the *A. biru* of the same author, which the writer of the article 'Kingfisher,' in the Penny Cyclopædia erroneously identifies with it. This species (from new Guinea) appears very closely allied to *A. azurea.*

Plate XXVI

Leonard lith.

Printed by Reeve Brothers

BUCCO VIRIDIS

ORD. INSESSORES.

TRIBE—SCANSORES.

GEN. BUCCO.

PLATE XXVI.

BUCCO VIRIDIS,

GREEN BARBET.

Synon.—*B. Viridis,* L., Jerd. Cat. No. 217 in part—*Le Barbu vert,* Buff—*Le Barbu de Mahé,* P. E.

The genus *Bucco,* as at present limited, is a well marked one, and appears confined to India and the Eastern Isles. Green is the predominant colour, both of the upper and lower surface, varied, according to the species, about the head and neck, with other colours, sometimes most brilliant.

The present species belongs to a small group, of which there are at least three species in continental India, distinguished by the plain brown and white markings of the head and neck. They abound in all the large forests, where their loud voice *Kŏturr, K'turr, Kotūrr,* may be heard ringing through the woods for a vast distance, throughout most of the day. They feed chiefly on fruit, also on insects; and, like parrots and woodpeckers, intermediate to which they appear to be, they breed in holes of trees, laying, I am informed, three or four white eggs. They are almost always seen singly, a pair, however, being usually not being far from each other.

The species figured on the plate is chiefly found in the woods on the Neilgherries, but also here and there in the forests of Malabar, chiefly in the higher portions of the Ghauts. Its note is hardly so loud as that of its more common congener of the Malabar forests, viz. *B. Zeylanicus.* Its flight, as indeed is that of all the species, is rapid, direct, and somewhat undulating. It perches generally on lofty branches of trees, and on a wood being beaten for game, several of these may be seen winging their way over the tops of the trees to a more secure spot.

I suspect that the call of this bird, or of the *B. Zeylanicus,* was mistaken for that of *Nyctiornis Athertoni* by the discoverer of that bird, as related in Jardine and Selby's Ill.

Orn. pl. 58; for it is described as being exactly the call of a *Bucco*, whilst that of the *Nyctiornis* is a loud rolling whistle. I have also heard the call of the *Bucco* by moonlight occasionally, but never that of the *Nyctiornis*.

I add a description of the Green Barbet. Head and neck above brown, sometimes tinged or rather edged with greenish; superciliary stripe, mark from the gape extending over the ears, throat and neck, yellowish white, the feathers of the lower part of the neck edged with brown; rest of the plumage bright green, darkest above, and paling beneath; bill, and naked skin round eye, brown; tarsus leaden colour; quills brown on the inner web only, except the first three which are edged with green.

Length about $8\frac{1}{2}$ inches, of wing 4, tail $2\frac{1}{2}$, tarsus 1, bill (at front) $\frac{8}{10}$ths, (at gape) $1\frac{2}{10}$ths.

Plate XXVII

R. E. B. lith.

Printed by Reeve Brothers.

RUFOUS BUZZARD
Buteo rufiventer

ORD. RAPTORES.

FAM. BUTEONIDÆ.

GEN. BUTEO.

PLATE XXVII.

BUTEO RUFIVENTER,

RUFOUS BUZZARD.

Synon.—*B. Rufiventer*, Jerdon Cat.—No. 21 bis. Suppl.

I have only obtained this species of Buzzard on the Neilgherries, where indeed it is very rare, as I only procured two specimens, one of which was seated on the edge of a swamp, and the other on a solitary tree on the side of a hill. It does not appear to frequent woods. The stomach of one I procured contained the remains of a lizard. I have occasionally seen one of the kind seated near the lake of Ootacamund, and a marsh in the neighbourhood, and fancy that it occasionally at least feeds on frogs.

I know nothing else of its habits, nor even if it is a permanent resident on the hills. In plumage it is closely allied to Hodgson's fine *Buteo canescens*, my *longipes*.

I add a brief description of its plumage. Above pale brown, each feather edged with rufous, especially on the head and neck; rump and upper tail coverts uniform brown; tail pale rufous, with narrow brown bars, the last widest; quills grey brown, white on the inner web with brown bars, except at the tip, beneath nearly pure white, forming a conspicuous broad white patch on the centre of the closed wing; cheeks and throat whitish, each feather centred rufous brown; rest of plumage beneath bright rufous or chesnut, barred with white; thigh coverts darker and not barred. Irides brown—cere and legs yellow.

Length about 21 inches, wing 15, tail 8, bill (at gape) $1\frac{4}{10}$, tarsus $3\frac{2}{10}$, wings reach nearly to the end of the tail.

Plate XXVIII

Leonard, lith

Reeve imp London

FALCO PEREGRINATOR.

ORD. RAPTORES.

FAM. FALCONIDÆ.

GEN. FALCO.

PLATE XXVIII.

FALCO PEREGRINATOR,

THE SHAHEEN FALCON.

Synon.—*F. Shaheen,* Jerdon Cat. No. 29, and Ill. Ind. Orn. Pl. xii. q. v.

At Plate XII. of the present work I gave a figure of the male of the present fine Falcon, under the name of *F. Shaheen*. It is only quite recently, since indeed the publication of Mr. Gray's list of the Raptores of the British museum, that it has been ascertained by British Ornithologists to have been described by Sundevall, a Swedish Naturalist who visited Calcutta, under the name now applied to it. I am much inclined to consider that the figure of the Falcon in the Pl. Enl. 469 was taken from a *Shaheen,* but this is said to have been European, and the *Shaheen* has not to my knowledge been hitherto enumerated, except in the Fauna of India, though I have little doubt that it extends far west, throughout Asia at all events.

The present figure was taken from a living trained female in my possession, that had completed one moult. The subsequent changes consist in the whole of the spots on the lower surface gradually disappearing, and in the upper plumage becoming lighter, and more slaty in hue.

Dimensions of a female are as follows: length about 18½, wing 13½, tail 6¼. With reference to the *addendum* at the end of my first Number, I may state that the *F. guttatus* there alluded to is not the Shaheen.

Plate XXIX.

Leonard lith.

Printed by Reeve Brothers

ACCIPITER BESRA.

ORD. RAPTORES.

FAM. ACCIPITRINÆ.

GEN. ACCIPITER.

PLATE XXIX.

ACCIPITER BESRA.

THE ADULT BESRA HAWK.

For Synon.—vide Plate IV.

The accompanying is another representation of a bird previously figured, but in a different state of plumage, and has moreover the advantage of having been figured from the living bird, a female, after her first moult. Shikarees state that it does not vary except in intensity of shade from the plumage exhibited in future moults.

I am confident that it will prove to be a distinct and well marked species. The specific name *minutus* of Latham, I believe, was originally given to a species killed in Malta, most probably an African one ; and the Malayan *virgatus*, with which it is supposed identical by Strickland, is a very distinct, though nearly allied species. For an account of dimensions, habits, &c. see Plate IV. of the present Illustrations.

Plate XXX.

R. E. B. lith.

Printed by Reeve Brothers.

STRIX CANDIDA, Tickell.

ORD. RAPTORES.

FAMILY STRIGIDÆ.

GENUS STRIX.

PLATE XXX.

STRIX CANDIDA.

LONG-LEGGED GRASS OWL.

Synon.—S. *Longimembris*—Jerdon, Cat. No. 38, S. *Candida,* Tickell, S. *Javanica* apud Blyth.

When I named this Owl as new, I had only met with a single specimen, which was shot on the Neilgherries near Coonoor. Since that time I have obtained other specimens, in the Nellore district, once in long grass when hunting for florikin, and again among long reeds in the dry bed of the tank at Yeroor, which had been fired to drive out some wild hog we were in search of.

On comparing it again with Tickell's description I find it agrees well enough, except as to the tarsi, which are said to be 'denuded,' but I imagine that he only meant it as comparatively so with *flammeus,* and as he especially mentions the fact of its being found only in long grass, I have now little doubt that they are identical, and have accordingly adopted his name. Mr. Blyth appears to think it may have been the species mentioned by Latham as S. *Javanica,* Gm. and de Wurmb, but I doubt much if it be the original species from Java. It was known to Buchanan, but Mr. Blyth has not obtained it from Bengal as yet.

The present figure was taken from a living specimen.

I add a description. Upper plumage generally brown, mixed with yellow, and spotted with white. Beneath white, tinged with ochreous, and spotted with brown. Face white, with a dark spot at the inner angle of the eye. Quills and tail barred with buff and brown ; some of the secondaries blotched with white ; bill pink, legs reddish brown. Irides dark brown, lower part of the tarsus nearly denuded of feathers.

Length about 17 inches, of wing 14, tail $5\frac{1}{4}$, tars. $3\frac{6}{10}$, middle toe $2\frac{1}{4}$, extent of wings 46.

The species of Owl figured by Dr. A Smith in his Zoology of South Africa as S. *Capensis* much resembles this in colours and structure.

Plate XXXI.

Leonard lith.

Printed by Reeve Brothers.

BRACHYPUS PARVICEPHALUS.

ORD. INSESSORES.

FAM. MERULIDÆ

SUB.-FAM. BRACHYPODINÆ.

GEN. BRACHYPODIUS—BL.

PLATE XXXI.

BRACHYPODIUS POIOICEPHALUS.

WHITE-EYED BULBUL.

Synon—*Brachypus Poioicephalus.*—Jerdon, Cat. No. 70.

I only once procured this species of Bulbul in forest at the foot of the Persia pass leading from Malabar into Wynaad.—It was feeding in small flocks on the tops of high trees, and I found had been eating berries.

Lord A. Hay procured one specimen at the foot of the Coonoor pass, and Captain Roberts of the 36th N. I. showed me a drawing of this bird, which he had procured on the West coast.

It is somewhat allied in colours to the *Brachypus eutilotus* of Jardine and Selby, which it further resembles in the copiousness of its rump feathers, and Mr. Blyth has classed them in the same genus.

Description.—Crown of head, occiput, and throat, bluish grey, forehead siskin green; back, wings, and lower plumage oil green, lighter towards the vent; rump feathers light yellowish green, broadly barred with black; tail with the centre feathers greenish grey, lateral feathers black at base terminated with grey; under tail coverts light grey. Irides bluish white; bill and legs greenish.

Length 7 inches, wing 3, tail 2 $\frac{8}{10}$ tars. $\frac{1}{2}$ inch, bill (at front) $\frac{4}{10}$ths.

Mr. Blyth, in a paper in the Journal Asiatic Society for 1845, page 546, has reviewed all the Indian *Brachipodinæ*, and has formed the genus *Brachipodius* (p. 576) for this and 4 or 5 other species.

Plate XXXII

Leonard lith. Printed by Reeve Brothers.

MUSCICAPULA SAPPHIRA. Blyth.

ORD. INSESSORES.

FAM. MUSCICAPIDÆ.

GEN. MUSCICAPULA.

PLATE XXXII.

MUSCICAPULA SAPPHIRA.

SAPPHIRE HEADED FLYCATCHER.

THE vast addition to the species of *Musoicapidæ* made of late, especially in India, having required a revision of the whole group, Mr. Blyth has recently* adopted several new genera, to one of which the subject of the present plate appertains. Mr. Blyth approximates it to the *Siphya* of Hodgson, from which, says he, it differs in its small size, and feeble legs and toes. I consider that its nearest affinity is with the group *Cyornis* of Blyth.

I add Mr. Blyth's description of the present bird, which was procured from the hill station of Darjeeling. Colour of the upper parts rich dark purplish blue, inclineing to ultramarine on the rump and upper tail coverts; forehead and crown vivid smalt blue; the lores black; foreneck and breast rich purple, with a broad median line of deep and bright ferruginous; flanks greyish, the belly and forepart of the wings underneath, with the axillaries, white; alars and tail black, edged with blue externally; bill and feet black.

Length 5 inch—wing $2\frac{1}{2}$—tail $1\frac{7}{8}$ths—bill to gape $\frac{9}{16}$ths—tarsus $\frac{5}{8}$ths.

* Journ. As. Soc. 1843, page 239, &c.

Plate XXXIII.

R. E. B. lith.

Printed by Reeve Brothers.

OTIS AURITA.

ORD. RASORES.

GEN. OTIS.

PLATE XXXIII.

OTIS AURITA.

THE BLACK FLORIKIN.

Synon.—*Otis Aurita—Passarage Bustard*—Latham, No. 13, perhaps *O. Indica ?—O. fulva*—Sykes—*O. Bengalensis,* apud Lesson—but not of older Authors—*O. Gularis*—Do.

MAJOR Franklin and Colonel Sykes in their Catalogues of the birds of Central India and the Deccan, having pronounced the common *Florikin* of India to be a distinct species from the Black one, I entered at some length, in my Catalogue of the birds of Southern India, into the reasons which led me to conclude that the views entertained by these writers were erroneous, and showed that the *Black Florikin* was nothing more than the cock-bird in the summer or breeding plumage. Since that article was written, I have had considerable additional experience, and every thing has tended to corroborate that opinion, and I may state, not only in my own estimation, but in that of almost every sportsman of experience with whom I have conversed on the subject. Some gentlemen were at first inclined to doubt this change, fancying it an anomaly, but when I pointed out that many of the birds of England underwent a similar periodical change, and that the *Golden Plover* assumed every summer a plumage nearly identical with that of the *Black Florikin,* they no longer hesitated to concur in my views.

My reasons for believing the Black and the common Florikin to be one and the same bird, may be here briefly recapitulated.

1stly. All *Black Florikin* hitherto examined have been male birds.

2ndly. The *Black Florikin* agrees exactly in size, and comparative dimensions, with the male of the *common Florikin,* as described fully by Colonel Sykes, but more especially in the length of wing, and acumination of the primary quills, the points insisted on by him, and most correctly so, as the essential points of difference from the female.

running or feeding. Its flesh is very delicate, and of excellent flavour, and it is the most esteemed here of all the game birds. Its pursuit is consequently a favorite sport, and from the open nature of the ground it frequents, it is well adapted for being hawked. I have killed it occasionally with the *Luggur*, but generally with the *Shaheen*, and have already (at Plate xii) given an account of the manner of hunting it. Should the *Shaheen* miss her first stoop, I have seen the *Florikin* accelerate its speed so greatly, that the falcon was unable to come up with it again under 600 yards or so. I have seen one struck dead by the *Wokhab*, *Aquila Vindhiana;* I had slipped a Luggur at it, which was in hot pursuit, though at some little distance behind, when two of these Eagles came down from a vast height, and joined in the chase. One of them made a headlong swoop at it, which the *Florikin* most skilfully avoided, only however to fall a victim to the talons of the other, which stooped almost immediately after its confederate, and dashed the poor bird lifeless to the ground. It had not, however, time to pick it up, for I rode up, and the Eagles soared off most unwillingly, and circled in the air long above me. The *Florikin* had its back laid open the whole length. The Luggur on seeing the Eagles join the chase, gave up at once and returned to the falconer's fist.

The *Florikin* is occasionally snared by some of the bird-catchers, but as this is a very uncertain process for catching a bird of such wandering habits, the gun is had resort to in general, and considerable numbers are brought into the markets in the districts where they abound—and fetch from half a rupee to a rupee each.

The *Florikin* is called by the Mussulmans of Southern India *Churz.* Latham I see gives this name, calling it *Churrus* and *Cirris*, which indeed is much the pronounciation of the word. In the Telinga language it is sometimes called, I am informed, *Kāmi-lēdi-pitta*, but generally *nela-nemili*, or ground Peacock; the Mahratta name, *Tun-mōr*, having exactly the same meaning, and in Hardwicke's notes (says Latham) the *Otis Bengalensis*, also called *Florikin* in Bengal, and *Churz* in Hindustani, is called in Sanscrit *Trīna mayara*, (properly *Trina mayūra*) which means grass Peacock. Its Tamool name I have already given. Its name in Canarese is *Kun-nowl*, which has much the same signification. It appears that the Bengal sportsmen apply the word *Florikin* only to the large *O. Bengalensis*, since named *deliciosa* by Gray, and *Himalayanus* by Vigors; and they call our bird the *leek*, or lesser *Florikin.* The origin of the word *Florikin* is not exactly known, but I have heard that either it, or *Flanderkin*, was the old English name for the little bustard of Europe. Latham gives, on the authority of various drawings, the Native name *Oorail*, which I have not heard; *Chulla Churz*, *Ab-*

luk-cherui, which means *Pied bird*, and *Flercher* in English. This latter is, I think, evidently of the same origin as *Florikin*. Others (says he) call it the *Passarage Plover*, which is the name applied to it in Pennant's Hindostan, where there is a figure of it. In one drawing it was called *Tok-dar ;* which, however, is the name of the Bustard, *O. Nigriceps*. An indifferent figure of the *Black Florikin*, in a state of change, is given at Plate X. of the Zoology of the Voyage of Belanger. Lesson, the author of the article, says that he does not know a figure of the adult *O. Aurita*, (though it had been previously I believe figured in Jardine and Selby's Illustrations of Ornithology) and that a specimen did not exist in the public collections of Paris. He also asserts its identity with *O. Gularis* and *Bengalensis* of the French Museum, and of some modern authors, and then says, "Thus the *Otis Bengalensis* is evidently only the *O. Aurita* without its ear tufts (palettes). It is the *Like* of the Hindoos." I know not on what authority he alleges this. On referring to Latham's account of *O. Bengalensis*, he gives its height 22 inches, and weight 12 to 14lb, &c. &c., so there can, I think, be very little doubt that the *O. Aurita* is not intended. Buffon too calls it (the *Bengalensis*,) the *Churge* or *L'Outarde Moyenne* des Indes, expressly because it is intermediate in size between the great and little Bustard of Europe.—Latham's *Black Headed Bustard*, No. 6, is perhaps meant for our bird.

I shall now give a short description of both male and female.

Length of the male bird from 18 to 19 inches—wing about 8—tail 4—tarsus barely 4—bill (at front) $1\frac{3}{10}$ths—weight 16 to 18 oz.

When in full breeding plumage, the head ear-tufts, neck, medial wing coverts, and lower plumage are deep black; chin, lower part of hind neck, and a large patch on the wing, white; the rest of the plumage dark brown, mottled with fulvous; the first three quills dusky brown, the remainder light fulvous yellow, barred and mottled with brown. The ear-tufts usually three in number on each side, and four inches long, rise from the lower portion of the ear coverts.

Irides pale yellowish, clouded with dusky. Bill dusky above, with the edges of the upper and all the lower mandible yellowish. Legs and feet dirty whitish yellow.

The female measures from $19\frac{1}{2}$ to 21 inches—wing $9\frac{3}{4}$—tail nearly 5—tarsus $4\frac{1}{2}$—bill (at front) $1\frac{1}{2}$—weighs 20 to 24 oz.

The prevalent color of her plumage is pale fulvous yellow, the feathers on the head, back, wings and tail, clouded and barred with deep brown—those on the head almost quite brown; foreneck with two irregular interrupted streaks, increasing on lower neck, and breast, lower plumage thence being unspotted and almost white;

hind neck finely speckled with brown; chin and throat white. First three quills almost entirely dark brown, the subsequent ones fulvous, barred with brown; wing coverts with only a few small bars of brown.

The male in winter plumage differs from the female only in always (I believe) having the shoulders and part of the wing coverts partially white, and in the under wing coverts being dark brown, whilst in the female they are pale fulvous, some lengthened feathers of the sides alone being brown in her.

The down at the base of all the feathers is pale pink, and the feather of the wing when freshly moulted, have a beautiful bloom on them, partly pink, and partly greenish. The quills are much narrowed, and in the male exceedingly acuminated, sometimes ending in a point almost as fine as that of a needle, as Colonel Sykes first pointed out; and this, with the smaller dimensions of wing, tarsus, &c., will always point out to the sportsman the sex of the bird he has shot. Colonel Sykes also mentions that the feathers of the back and scapulars are triangular at the point.

The *Florikin* of Southern India has, I see, been lately placed in a new sub-genus of *Otis*, named *Sypheotides* by Lesson, a division, which the smaller size of the male, its ear-tufts, and other peculiarities perhaps would warrant us in adopting. I have not seen any account of a similar difference between the sexes of any of the African small Bustards, and in the European little Bustard as well as in the large Bustards of Europe and India, the male bird is much the largest of the two.

I see it mentioned in Yarrell's British Birds, that the little Bustard of Europe also undergoes a periodical change in the breeding season, assuming a black collar on the neck, with a white gorget and ring.

Plate [illegible]

B. K. B. lith. Reeve imp. London.

ANAS CARYOPHYLLACEA.

ORD. NATATORES.

FAM. ANATIDÆ.

GENUS ANAS.

PLATE XXXIV.

ANAS CARYOPHYLLACEA.

PINK HEADED DUCK.

Syn.—*A. Caryophyllacea,* Latham Ind. Orn.—*Le Millouin ā cou rose.*—Lesson, Traité, No. 40.

I inserted this Duck in my Catalogue of Indian Birds on the authority of some Shikarees at Jalnah, who described it accurately as being a rare visitant to that neighbourhood. Lesson inserts it in his 'Traité' as existing in the Paris Museum, though Swainson* says he had never heard of a specimen dead or alive in England.

Since my Catalogue was published I have obtained two specimens, one from the Nellore district, and the other (in imperfect plumage) in the Madras Market. It must however be considered a very rare kind, even in the North of India, as Mr. Blyth has but seldom procured it. Latham says that it is common in Oude, and lives generally in pairs, is often kept tame, and becomes tolerably familiar. I should be glad if any Sportsmen would communicate to me instances of its occurrence here.

I add a description—head, cheeks, sides, and hind neck, pale pink or rose colour; the rest of the plumage of a glossy reddish brown, somewhat paler beneath; speculum and inner webs of quills pale reddish fawn; edge of the wing white; some of the tertiaries lengthened and glossy green—bill red—legs leaden.

Length about 24 inches—Wing $10\frac{1}{2}$—Tail 4—Tarsus $1\frac{8}{16}$th—Bill at gape $2\frac{1}{2}$.

* Animals in Menageries, p. 277.

Plate XXXV

Leonard lith

Reeve Brothers London

PYCNONOTUS XANTHOLÆMUS.

ORD. INSESSORES.

FAM. BRACHYPODINÆ.

GEN. PYCNONOTUS.

PLATE XXXV.

PYCNONOTUS XANTHOLÆMUS.

YELLOW THROATED BULBUL.

In the second Supplement to my Catalogue of Indian Birds just published, I have described this Bird, which was brought me from the Eastern range of Ghauts dividing Cuddapah from the Nellore district, by some excellent hill Shikarees to whom I am indebted for more than one novelty. They describe it as frequenting the densest woods in elevated valleys, and assert that it lives chiefly on fruit of various kinds. The name they apply to it is *Konda poda pigli*, or hill bush bulbul, the name *poda pigli* being always applied to *Pycnonotus flavirictus* (my *Tricophorus virescens*).

I have not seen specimens from any other part of the country.

Description—crown of head yellowish green; throat and fore-neck pale yellow; upper plumage ashy, tinged with green, especially on wings and tail; beneath pale ashy, under tail coverts and lower tibial plumes, yellow; tail feathers, except the centre ones, tipped with whitish, the external most broadly so—Bill black; legs and feet dark plumbeous; irides said to be red.

Length nearly 8 inches—wing $3\frac{6}{10}$th—Tail $3\frac{1}{2}$—Tarsus $\frac{8}{10}$th—Bill at front $\frac{6}{10}$th—at gape $\frac{8}{10}$th.

Plate XXXVI

R.E.B. lith.

Printed by Reeve Brothers.

PTEROCLES QUADRICINCTUS. Female.

ORD. RASORES.

FAM. TETRAONIDÆ.

GEN. PTEROCLES.

PLATE XXXVI.

PTEROCLES QUADRICINCTUS.

PAINTED ROCK-GROUSE.

FEMALE.

A FIGURE of the male bird, with a full account of its habits, having already appeared at Plate X. of the present work, I can only add here, that it is said to be identical with the bird from Western Africa. I have had this bird in confinement for a few days, and its call when alarmed was very grouse-like.

Description.—Plumage generally ochreous yellow, (the feathers when fresh moulted having a strong tinge of pink) spotted and barred with dark brown; beneath pale ashey, finely barred with brown; quills as in the male bird.

Plate XXXVII

Leonard lith. Reeve Brothers London.

BRACHYPUS RUBINEUS.

ORD. INSESSORES.

FAM. BRACHYPODINÆ.

GEN. BRACHYPUS.

PLATE XXXVII.

BRACHYPUS RUBINEUS.

RUBY THROATED BULBUL.

Synon.—*Brachypus Gularis.*—Gould, Proc. Zoo. Soc.—1835.

I HAVE only found the Ruby Throated Bulbul in Malabar, generally in open glades of the forest, and in the neighbourhood of water, frequenting trees and bushes in small flocks, and feeding on various fruits and berries. It is certainly a rare bird, though I have seen it in one or two collections made in Malabar and Travancore.

Sometime ago I suggested to Mr. Blyth that it may have been Gould's species *Gularis,* described from Travancore, but the description of the throat is omitted, probably through mistake, as the specific name is derived therefrom. Mr. Blyth in his synopsis of the Brachypodinæ, before alluded to,* has made a new genus for this and Horsfield's *Turdus dispar,* (which closely resembles our bird) under the name of *Rubigula.*

Description.—Head and cheeks pure glossy black; plumage above, yellowish green; chin spot black; throat of a beautiful shining ruby red, the feathers divided, and somewhat bristly; rest of the plumage beneath, yellow; quills with their inner webs dusky, bill black, legs greenish dusky, irides light yellow.

Length about $6\frac{1}{2}$—wing 3—tail $2\frac{3}{4}$—tarsus $\frac{6}{10}$ths.

* I. A. S. 1845, p. 576.

Plate XXXVIII

R.E.B. lith. Printed by Reeve Brothers

MIRAFRA ERYTHROPTERA.

ORD. INSESSORES.

TRIBE CONIROSTRES.

FAM. ALAUDINÆ.

GEN. MIRAFRA.

PLATE XXXVIII.

MIRAFRA ERYTHROPTERA.

RED WINGED LARK.

Synon.—*Mirafra Javanica?* Jerdon, Cat. No. 189.

WHEN I compiled my Catalogue I placed this Lark, though with doubt, as the *M. Javanica* of Horsfield, that bird having been included in Franklin's Catalogue, and as it answered tolerably well to the brief description. I think it is probably the variety of Latham's *Aggia Lark*, No. 49, described after a drawing of Hardwicke's, and said to weigh 9½ drachms. Since that time, however, I have thought it advise-able to separate it as a new species, and Mr. Blyth fully agrees with me in doing so, and has already described it under that name in the Journ. Asiat. Soc.*

The Red Winged Lark is tolerably common in low jungles in the neighbour-hood of Jalnah, and generally through the Deccan. I never saw it south of Bellary nor on the West Coast, nor in the Carnatic, until a short time ago, when I observed it in some low jungle at the very base of the Eastern Ghats, and my Shikarees have procured me specimens from the hilly regions, where they say it abounds. It is never, that I am aware of, found in the open plains, nor does it frequent gardens, like the more common species, *M. Affinis.* I may remark here, that I found this latter the common species, within a mile or less of the spot where I first observed *Erythroptera* in the Carnatic, but not one did I see encroaching on the ground of the other. The Red Winged Lark perches frequently on shrubs, whence it occasionally rises a short distance, and descends again with outspread wings, its bright rufous quills glittering

* For 1844—Page 958.

in the sun. When observed it hides itself behind a bush, and if followed, soon contrives to conceal itself from the sportsman.

Description.—Above dusky reddish brown, the feathers edged with fulvous; beneath fulvous white, the breast spotted with brown; feathers of the head lengthened and rufous; chin, throat, and superciliary streak, white; quills bright ferruginous on both webs, except at the tip, which is dusky brown; tail dark brown, the feathers edged with lighter, and the outermost one white on its external web. Bill horny brown—irides brown—legs and feet fleshy yellow.

Length about $5\frac{1}{2}$ inches—wing $3\frac{2}{10}$ths—tail $2\frac{1}{10}$ths—tarsus $\frac{3}{4}$ths, bill at front $\frac{4}{10}$ths.

This and another species are called in Teloogoo *Eeli jitta*, the present one, distinguished by its smaller size, being called *chinna eeli jitta.* The name is derived from their note, which in both species is a kind of prolonged whistle. The nearly allied species, *M. Affinis*, differs in having the quills rufous on the outer web, and the basal half only with a deep margin of the same, in its shorter tail, and differently formed bill. It is exceedingly abundant in the West Coast, and throughout the Carnatic, frequenting open spaces in the jungles, gardens, &c. &c. Mr. Strickland considers that this may be the *Alauda Malabarica* of the older authors, described from Sonnerat's voyage, plate 113, fig. 1; and I accordingly inserted it in the 2d supplement to my Catalogue just published,* under that name; but having again compared the description, I agree with Mr. Blyth in applying this term to the crested lark, *Alauda-deva* of Sykes, which is not uncommon on the Malabar Coast, and shall retain the name of *Affinis*, already indeed published by Mr. Blyth.

* Madras Journal of Literature and Science, No. 31.

Plate XXXIX

Leonard, Lith

Printed by Reeve Brothers, London.

DICÆUM CONCOLOR.

ORD. INSESSORES.

TRIBE TENUIROSTRES.

GEN. DICÆUM.

PLATE XXXIX.

DICÆUM CONCOLOR.

OLIVE FLOWER PECKER.

This plain coloured little bird is found in great abundance on the Neilgherries, frequenting mostly high trees in small flocks, and feeding chiefly on the minute insects that infest flowers, occasionally receiving a portion of honey along with the insects. I have also found it not uncommon in the more open parts of the forests of Malabar, and also occasionally in jungles in the Carnatic, when a little more high and dense than usual. It keeps up an incessant feeble twittering, whilst feeding. It appears to be replaced towards the North of India by another species, *Dicæum erythrorhynchum*, the *Nectarinia Minima* of Tickell, and *Dicæum Tickelliæ* olim of Blyth; of which, however, I have recently obtained specimens from Canara. My Shikarees call this little bird *chitloo jitta*, a name which they also apply to that curious bird the *Parisoma Vireoides* of my Cat. No. 133; the *Fringilla Agilis* of Tickell, and *Pipra Squalida* of Burton, now made into a new genus, *Piprisoma*,* by Mr. Blyth, and placed in the *Dicæum* group by him; thus confirming the view of its affinities held by my Shikarees, which I confess it was some time before I could recognise.

I add a description of the *Dicæum Concolor*. Above brownish olive, wings and tail darker, beneath greenish white, irides brown. Bill dark plumbeous, legs and feet brown. Length about 4 inches—wing $2\frac{1}{10}$—tail $1\frac{1}{10}$—tarsus $\frac{1}{2}$—bill (front) $\frac{4}{10}$ths, at gape $\frac{5}{10}$ths.

The bird is figured on the branch of a tree well known on the Neilgherries under the name of the pink arbutus, which is I believe a species of *Thibaudia*.

Plate XL.

Picus Cordatus

ORD. INSESSORES.

TRIBE SCANSORES.

FAM. PICIDÆ.

GEN. HEMICIRCUS.

PLATE XL.

HEMICIRCUS CORDATUS.

HEART-SPOTTED WOODPECKER.

Syn.—*Picus cordatus,* Jerdon Cat. No. 206.—*P. canente,* Lesson, Centurie Zoologique Pl. 73?

I can hardly bring myself to believe that the Woodpecker figured in the plate, is the same as the one described by Lesson as follows—"This Woodpecker has neither red nor green in its plumage; two colours only, black and white form its plumage; crest, head and hind neck, deep blue-black.—Throat and foreneck ashy grey, relieved on each side by two broad white marks, reaching from the commissure of the bill to the upper part of the thorax. All the lower part of the body from the breast of a deep smoky brown." The uncoloured figure which accompanies my copy of Lesson's 'Centurie,' certainly shows a decided similarity in the appearance of the bird, and character of the markings, but assuming Lesson's description of the plumage to be correct, and taking into consideration the very different locality of his bird, I am inclined to the opinion that the *Picus canente* from Pegu is a distinct species from my *P. cordatus* from the forests of Malabar and Travancore. The attention now bestowed on the discrimination of species has had the result of showing that several Woodpeckers previously considered identical from different parts of India and Malayana, are in reality only representatives of each other in different districts.

For example three species, formerly considered the same, have been found to form the group of which the Malay *Picus badius* was the first described—viz. *P. badius verus*, from Malayana, *P. phaioceps*, from Bengal, and *P. gularis*, mihi, from Southern India. In like manner the group to which the Malayan *P. tiga* belongs has at least two representatives in Continental India, viz. *P. shorii* and *intermedius*. Two additional species have been added to the *Bengalensis* group, viz. *Micropus* from Southern India, and another from Scinde, as I have lately learned from Mr. Blyth, and other instances might readily be adduced. Now in all these cases the distinctions though constant, are apparently very trifling, and only appreciable after a close examination, in some cases being merely structural. I am therefore led to conclude in the absence of actual comparison of specimens from Pegu that my *P. cordatus* is the continental representative of *canente*, and a distinct species. A nearly allied species has quite recently been procured by Mr. Blyth from Arracan which he has named *jugularis*.

The heart-spotted Woodpecker is found only in the highest forests of Malabar, Travancore, and Canara, frequenting high trees, usually in pairs, or single. Like Woodpeckers generally it is a wary bird, and being constantly in motion, occasionally eludes the pursuit of the naturalist. Though generally spread through the forests of Western India, it is a rare bird. Collections made on the West Coast however usually include it. I have not seen it myself from any other part of the country, but Mr. Blyth, I think, has obtained specimens from Assam or Arracan.

Description—Male—forehead and crown, chin, throat and cheeks, back, stripe along the wings, and tertiaries yellowish white, the latter terminated with a black heart-shaped spot. Hind head and long occipital crest, nape, scapulars, quills, upper and under tail coverts, vent and tail deep black. Beneath from throat to the vent dull green. On the centre of the back is a brush of dark sap green feathers, rough and bristly, and usually smeared with a viscid secretion. Bill blackish—legs and feet greenish black—irides brown red.

The female differs only in having the forehead and crown black, dotted with yellowish white.

Length under 6 inches—Wing $3\frac{3}{4}$—Tail 1 [illegible]th—Tarsus [illegible]th—Bill (at front) $\frac{5}{10}$th to [illegible]th—Crest long; form peculiarly robust; feet large; wings long.

Miller lith. Reeve (London) imp.

SCOPS TUNIA.

ORD. RAPTORES.

FAM. STRIGIDÆ.

GEN. SCOPS.

PLATE XLI.

SCOPS SUNIA.

RED SCOPS OWL.

Synon.—*Scops sunia*—Hodgson, As. Res. xix. 174. *Sc. pennata* H., apud Jerdon, 2d Suppl. Cat.

When I referred this bird to *S. pennata* of Hodgson, I did so on the ground of the great similarity of one of the states of plumage of this beautiful little Owl to an imperfect specimen of *pennata* kindly lent me by Mr. Blyth. Mr. Gray of the British Museum now refers *pennata* to the European Scops Owl, *S. zorca*, though he previously placed it as distinct; and on again examining this species I recognise many points of distinction between the two birds, viz., *sunia* and *zorca*. Mr. Blyth has obtained several specimens in the neighbourhood of Calcutta, all in the red state of plumage, and naturally doubts any change taking place, at least normally. The fact of this change is well established I believe in the American Scops Owl, figured by Wilson, and as the majority of specimens I have obtained were in the grey plumage, and some much more rufous than others, I am myself confident of the identity of the two birds. Whether, however, the red be the young plumage, as in the American species, or the adult, I cannot determine satisfactorily, but I suggest that it may be a seasonal garb, and shall endeavour to ascertain this.

This Owl appears to be widely distributed through India. The first specimen I procured was found dead in my compound at Madras. I have since seen specimens from Malabar and Travancore, and obtained several others from the Eastern Ghats near Nellore. Mr. Blyth has got it at Calcutta, and Mr. Hodgson in Nepal, but it has not yet I believe been sent from any of the Malay Countries. It is stated to be quite nocturnal in its habits, and to live chiefly on insects. Mr. Hodgson's specific name is derived from the native, meaning *golden*, and Telinga Shikarees called it *Chitta Gooba.*

I shall now give descriptions of the different states of plumage—1st. The uniform rufous as figured. In this the whole of the upper parts are bright ferruginous, a few only of the feathers with black shafts. Scapulars white, tipped with black—feathers of the ruff also edged with black—beneath white, much tinged with rufous on the breast, least so on the under tail coverts, the feathers with a black central stripe, and cross markings—quills and tail obscurely dark banded. 2d. Another state differs from this in having the central black streak and cross markings fully developed on all the feathers, and the quills and tail darker banded. A third state has the ground colour of a beautiful *pale grey*, but with the markings as in the last, here and there generally a little rufous still discernible, especially on the wings and tail—as also on the aigrettes and ruff.

Length $6\frac{1}{2}$ inches to 7—the wing is $5\frac{2}{10}$ths, and the tail is $2\frac{4}{10}$ths—tarsus $\frac{8}{10}$ths.

I shall notice here that this old established generic name Scops has been lately changed at home for *Ephialtes*, the former being now applied to the crowned Cranes.

Plate XLII

Miller lith. Reeve (London) imp.

FRANCOLINUS HARDWICKII.

ORD. RASORES.

FAM. TETRAONIDÆ.

GEN. FRANCOLINUS.

PLATE XLII.

FRANCOLINUS HARDWICKII—FEMALE.

FEMALE PAINTED SPUR-FOWL.

Synon.—*Perdix benulasa*, Val., *P. Hardwickii*, Gray, Hardw. Ill. Ind. Zool. *F. nivosus*, Ad. Delessert, *Curria Partridge*, Latham—*Jitta Kodee*, Teloogoo.

THE male of this very handsome Spur-fowl has been figured twice, firstly by Gray in Hardwicke's Illustrations of Indian Zoology, and afterwards by Delessert in the Magasin de Zoologie—but the hen-bird has, I believe, not yet been described. Mr. Blyth I see gives *benulasa* Val. as the prior specific appellation.

In Southern India I have only found it in the Jungles of the Eastern Ghats, and in some of the spurs that jut out from the Ghats, both above and below. M. Delessert got it from the neighbourhood of Pondicherry. I got many specimens from the Ghats inland from Nellore, and I have been told that it is found near Bellary, Cuddapah and Hydrabad. Further north I never saw it from Goomsoor, and it is unknown in Bengal and the Himalayas. General Hardwicke procured it in the North West of India I believe.

It associates in small flocks, keeping to the low shrubs and brushwood, and seeking its food among fallen leaves and low herbage. I kept several individuals of this species alive for some time, and found that it is a most pugnacious and quarrelsome bird. It carries its tail erect like the Jungle fowl, to which the natives invariably assert its affinity, as well as that of *F. spadiceus;* and Mr. Blyth places them in his genus *Gallo perdix*, retaining *Francolinus* for the common Partridge of India, *F. ponticerianus*, and the Black Partridge of Bengal, *F. communis*, which are much more allied to Partridges, and in which the hens are not usually spurred as in *Gallo perdix*.

I have found that both the spotted and common Spur-fowl feed much on insect food in the wild state, especially on the larvæ of two or three kinds of wood bug *(Reduvius)* so abundant in most of our Jungles.

Description.—Plumage generally of a dusky greenish brown, paling beneath, and inclining to fulvescent on the breast and abdomen. Top of head dark brown, with deep ferruginous streaks, of which latter colour are the face, superciliary stripe and chin, some of the feathers of this portion being centred with pale buff, which colour forms a marked streak extending from the base of the lower mandible to the ear. Bill horny brown. Legs cinereous.

Length about 12½ inches—wing 6—tail 5—tarsus 1½.

The Cock-bird differs in having the whole head and neck black with numerous white spots, the back and feathers of the leg fine chesnut also white spotted, each spot surrounded with glossy black, lower part of breast and abdomen buff, black spotted, lower tail coverts, wings, and tail brownish, the former slightly streaked white.

Plate XLIII

Miller lith. Reeve (London) imp.

CHLOROPSIS JERDONI.

ORD. INSESSORES.

FAM. BRACHYPODINÆ.

GEN. CHLOROPSIS.

PLATE XLIII.

CHLOROPSIS JERDONI.

COMMON GREEN BULBUL.

Synon.—*C. cochinsinensis*, apud Jerdon, Cat. No. 72. *Phyllornis Jerdoni*, Blyth Jour. As. Bengal 1844, page 392, and 1845, page 564.

It is somewhat remarkable that a species so extensively distributed, and by no means uncommon, and of which specimens must have been frequently taken home, should only within the last three years have been discriminated from its congeners. The cause of this is to be found partly in the great similarity of plumage of the birds of this very natural genus, and partly in the carelessness (till of late years) of Naturalists in unravelling synonyms. As Dr. Roxburgh received from some Critic on his magnificent work on Indian Plants most unmerited censure for figuring the *Roxburghia gloriosoides*, which name the ignorant writer attributed to Roxburgh himself, I beg to observe that I am indebted to Mr. Blyth for the honor of having this bird named after myself.

The genus was first defined (in England) and the known species recorded in Jardine and Selby's Illustrations of Ornithology. It appears, however, that *Phyllornis* of Müller has the priority, and must therefore hereafter be adopted.

The genus is peculiar to India and the Malayan provinces, and has been the cause of some discussion as to its place in the natural system. Mr. Blyth, among others, places it, along with *Jora*, as a particular sub-family of *Meliphagidæ*, peculiar to Southern Asia and its Islands, and Mr. Gray places it in his *Meliphaginæ*. Mr. Blyth, however, allows that it conducts to the Bulbuls, *Brachypodinæ*, in which family it is placed by Swainson; and it will be seen from the heading of this article, that I adopt this view, to which I am led partly by the habits of the bird, and partly by the geographical distribution. Its possession of a pencilled or brushed tongue, of which it does not make typical use, appears to me rather an analogical character, and its other alliances being confessedly with the Brachypodinæ, I have preferred placing it there.

The subject of the present article is spread over great part of the Continent of India, wherever there is a sufficiency of woodland. It is extremely common in all the Western provinces, and in the Jungles of the Eastern Ghats, but is rarely met with in the open country of the Carnatic, Mysore or Hydrabad, and there only in the vicinity of well wooded towns. It is usually to be met with in pairs, flitting about the extreme branches of trees, examining the leaves for various insects, after which it occasionally takes a short flight of a foot or two, or searching for some suitable fruit. It has a somewhat varied note, its usual call being, as Mr. Blyth remarks, not unlike that of the King Crow *(Dicrurus macrocercus,)* though softened down and mellowed, and occasionally is very agreeable. I have seen a nest and eggs of this species in possession of S. N. Ward, Esq. It is a neat but slight, cup-shaped nest composed chiefly of fine grass, and was placed near the extremity of a branch, some of the nearest leaves being, it was said, brought down and loosely surrounding it. It contained two eggs, white with a few claret-coloured blotches. Its nest and eggs, I may remark, show an analogy to that of the Orioles as mentioned in a previous article, Plate XV., which is also a representative among the true Thrushes of the Meliphagous or Tenuirostral tribes. The Orioles being by some, though not so generally, assigned to the *Meliphaghidæ*, this may seem an additional proof of the correctness of those who would place our bird in the same group, but I only see in it another proof of the universality of the principle of Representation, which pervades every tribe throughout the animated world.

Description.—Male, of the beautiful pale green colour prevalent throughout the genus. Face, chin, throat and gorge black, surrounded with a zone of pale yellowish green. Moustache, shining smalt blue. Shoulder-spot, shining azure blue. The female differs in having the parts that are black in the male of a light bluish green, and the moustachial streak azure blue.

Length from 7 to 7½ inches—wing 3½—tail 2¾—tarsus nearly $\frac{8}{10}$ths. Irides pale brown. Bill dusky. Legs cinereous.

The only other species met with on the Peninsula of India is the *C. Malabaricus*, (Lath.,) *C. cæsmarhynchos*, apud Tickell, *C. aurifrons* of my Cat. This species is much more rare than the last, preferring the vicinity of lofty Jungles, and is only to be found about the Western Coast, and some of the denser portions of the Jungles of the Eastern Ghats. It is nearly allied to the *C. aurifrons* of Northern India. A fourth very beautiful species, *C. Hardwickii*, J. and S., *C. Curvirostris*, Sw., *C. cyanopterus*, Hodgs., *C. chrysogaster*, McL. and H., and *C. auriventris*, Deless., is found in the Himalayas and Eastern India.

Three species are found in the Malay Peninsula and isles, viz., *C. Sonneratii*, J. and S., *C. cyanopogon*, T., and *C. cochinsinensis*, Lath.

ORD. RAPTORES.

FAM. FALCONINÆ.

GEN. FALCO.

PLATE XLIV.

FALCO LUGGUR.

THE LUGGUR FALCON.

Synon.—*F. juggur*—Gray—Hardwicke's Ill. Ind. Zool. 2—26. *F. thermophilus*, Hodgs.. Gray's Zool. Misc.

I HAVE already in these Illustrations figured two states of plumage of a fine Falcon, (the Shaheen,) and I now give a drawing of another equally large, much more common, and held in less estimation by the Natives. Whilst the Bhyree *(F. peregrinus,)* prefers the sea coast and the neighbourhood of lakes, rivers, and wet cultivation, and the Shaheen *(F. peregrinator)* delights in hilly and wooded regions, the Luggur, on the contrary, frequents open dry plains, and vicinity of cultivation. It makes its nest in some lofty tree, generally one standing alone among some grain fields, and lays four eggs. In a wild state it preys on a great variety of small birds, often snatching up a chicken, even in the midst of a Cantonment. It is trained to hunt Crows, Paddy-birds, Partridges and Florikin; and, it is said, has been trained to kill the Heron, *A. cinerea*.

In hawking Crows, *C. culminatus* chiefly, it is slipped from the hand; and the Crow, when aware of its danger, uses every artifice to escape, taking refuge among cattle, horses, vehicles, and even entering houses. I once had a *Luggur* whose wing-feathers were burnt off by a washerman's fire, close to which the Crow was attempting to take refuge when it was struck. After Paddy-birds *(Ardea bubulcus)* it is also slipped from the hand, and as this bird is always found on the plains feeding among herds of cattle, it affords considerable sport by its dexterity in diving among and under the cattle, and the venturous Hawk is occasionally trodden under the feet of the cattle. When the quarry is a Partridge or a Florikin the standing gait is used as described

Plate XLIV.

Miller lith.

Reeve (London) imp.

FALCO LUGGUR.

under the head of the Shaheen, (Plate XII.) Luggurs, as well as Shaheens, are always caught after they have left the nest and have had some instruction by their parents, our native Falconers considering them better than when taken from the nest, contrary I believe to the opinion of our English Adam Woodcocks. The Luggur appears to inhabit the whole continent of India—and is enumerated among the Hawks used in Scinde by the late Sir A. Burnes. I add a description of the Luggur and of its changes of plumage.

The young bird, as represented in the accompanying Plate, is throughout of an earth-brown colour, except the superciliary stripe, cheeks, chin, throat, and under-tail coverts, which are of a pale yellowish white colour, more marked in some individuals than in others, and in some of a purer white. The quills are darker than the rest of the plumage, and the tail has sometimes an ashy tinge. The head is usually, though not always, paler, sometimes quite rufous, and the feathers edged with creamy white, and the forehead is generally of this latter tinge. In the second year the brown feathers of the upper plumage are paler and with more of an ashy tinge throughout; beneath, the feathers of the neck and breast are snow white, with a central brown mark. In the third year still more of the breast, and part of the abdominal feathers become white, with a brown spot, this mark on the upper portion of the breast being now nearly obliterated; the feathers of the back too are now quite cinereous. In the fourth year the breast becomes quite white unspotted, a few brown spots still remaining on the abdomen—which disappear nearly with the next moult. In all the head is paler, sometimes rufous with a few dark lines. The leg feathers also always remain brown. The upper plumage is pale cinereous, usually edged with light brown, and the nape and hind neck always continue brown. The quills have at all ages their inner webs studded with large white spots. In the young bird the cere orbits and legs are light cinereous blue, which afterwards changes to yellow, pale at first, brighter with age. Irides deep brown.

Length of a female 19 inches—wing $15\frac{1}{4}$—tail 8—tarsus 2—centre toe with claw $2\frac{3}{4}$—weight lb$1\frac{1}{2}$. The male bird is considerably smaller, but there is not such a difference between the sexes as in the Peregrine and the Shaheen.

The Hindustani name of this Falcon is *Luggur* for the female, and *Juggur* for the male. In Teloogoo it is called *Luggadoo* evidently the same word.

Besides the *Shaheen*, *Luggur* and *Besra*, already figured in the present Illustrations, the following Hawks are known to, and used by native Falconers. 1st. The *Bhyree, Falco peregrinus.* An abundant visitant to our coasts during the cold season.

2d. The *Turoomtee*, *F. chicquera*, a permanent resident. 3d. The *Baz*, *Astur palumbarius*, rare in the South of India. 4th. The *Gorbesra*, *Astur indicus*, also rare. 5th. The *Basha*, *Accipiter fringillarius*, a cold weather visitant to hilly regions. 6th. The *Shikra*, *Acc. Dussumierii*, abundant throughout India—and lastly, the *Khandesra*, probably the *Acc. virgatus*—very rare, and said only to be found on the East coast.

Plate XLV.

Miller lith. Reeve (London) imp.

ANTHUS SIMILIS.

ORD. INSESSORES.

FAM. MOTACILLINÆ.

GEN. ANTHUS.

PLATE XLV.

ANTHUS SIMILIS—JERDON.

MOUNTAIN TITLARK.

The group of Larks, and Titlarks, is one of the most difficult to define of all the feathered tribes, their plumage being in general so extremely similar, that without accurate measurements and comparisons of allied species, numerous mistakes are unavoidable. Mr. Blyth has lately, in one of his excellent papers in the Journal of the Asiatic Society of Bengal, revised all the Indian species; and Mr. Gray, in his list of Hodgson's birds, has also enumerated several. The subject of our present article is certainly one of the rarest of all. It is not enumerated among Hodgson's birds, but I see that Lord A. Hay has lately obtained it at Jummoo in the North West Himalayas. My first specimens were procured at Jalna, in the neighbourhood of low hills on a bare plain. I have since, on several occasions, seen it on the Segoor Pass of the Neelgherries, among rocky ground about 4,000 feet high, and have little doubt that it will eventually be found to frequent rocky hills throughout the table land of India. I presume that it is a resident here, for I lately procured a specimen in what is evidently its nestling plumage on the Segoor Ghat.

Description.—Plumage above generally of a dusky olive brown, the feathers edged with pale ferruginous, darkest on the margins of the wing feathers; beneath, and superciliary stripe also pale ferruginous, streaked on the neck and breast with brown; outermost tail-feather with the outer web and tip rusty white, and the next tipped with the same only. Irides brown.

Length 8 inches—wing $3\frac{8}{10}$ths—tail $3\frac{1}{2}$—tarsus rather more than an inch—bill to forehead $\frac{6}{10}$ths—hind claw nearly $\frac{4}{10}$ths.

This species differs abundantly both in habits and structure from *A. Richardi*, (which equals it in size,) and is one of the best marked species of the group. Richard's Pipit frequents chiefly marshy ground, and wet paddy-fields, and in such localities is more abundant in Southern India than I previously imagined. Other Pipits found in the Peninsula are as follows—*A. maculatus*, Hodgs.; *A. arboreus*, of Indian writers, very abundant as a cold weather visitant; *A. striolatus*, Blyth, placed by Mr. Gray in his list as a synonym of *A. rufescens* of Europe. This species appears also to be only a cold weather visitant. I found it abundant on plains near Nellore sprinkled with bushes of Euphorbia, on which the Pipit frequently perched. *A. malayensis*, Eyton, *A. agilis*, Sykes, and Jerdon Cat., *A. pallescens*, apud Sundevall. A most abundant and common species throughout all India. *A. rufulus* of apud Jerdon, Cat. No. 192., lately obtained by Mr. Blyth near Calcutta—and lastly, *A. montana*, Jerdon, olim *A. rufescens*, Cat. No. 191—only seen on the Neelgherries, where tolerably common.

Plate XLVI.

Miller lith.

Reeve (London) imp.

PARUS NUCHALIS.

ORD. INSESSORES.

FAM. PARINÆ.

GEN. PARUS.

PLATE XLVI.

PARUS NUCHALIS.

WHITE NAPED TITMOUSE.

I OBTAINED this unexpected addition to the fauna of Southern India from the Jungles of the Eastern Ghats, and the Shikarees who brought it to me stated that it inhabits the highest portion of the hills in thick forest, and lives in pairs. They said it was very rare, and I have not succeeded in obtaining any other specimens beyond the pair first procured.

Description.—Above, and a broad mesial stripe from throat to vent, black; cheeks, sides of neck, of breast, and of belly, under-tail coverts, spot on nape and band across wing, white; tertials broadly margined externally and tipped with white; outermost tail-feather white, except its inner border, the next with the outer web and portion of inner web white, and the third with the outer web white at tip and for most of its basal half. Bill black. Legs plumbeous.

Length 5 inches—wing $2\frac{3}{8}$ths—tail 2—tarsus $\frac{5}{8}$ths—bill $\frac{1}{2}$ inch nearly to gape.

The other *Pari* of Southern India are *P. cinereus*, V., *P. atriceps*, T., abundant on the Neelgherries; and *P. aplonotus*, Blyth, *P. xanthogenys*, apud Sykes and Jerdon—only lately discriminated from the allied *P. xanthogenys* of the Himalayas. This is abundant in Coorg, on the slopes of the Neelgherries, and indeed all along the range of the Western Ghats. *P. melanolophus* I have only seen in Goomsoor.

ORD. INSESSORES.

FAM. PICIDÆ.

GEN. PICUS.

PLATE XLVII.

PICUS CEYLONUS.

RED WOODPECKER.

Synon.—*P. ceylonus*, Forst., *P. neglectus*, Wagler.

I HAVE figured this interesting species of Woodpecker from the island of Ceylon, where it was procured by Lord A. Hay, and where it appears to be not uncommon, replacing (says Mr. Blyth) the common *P. bengalensis* of the Indian continent, to which it assimilates in structure, belonging to the same division *Brachypternus*.

Description.—Above of a dull crimson colour, brighter on the head and crest —beneath white, with brown markings; streak from the eye and two narrow stripes, one from above the gape, and the other from the edge of the lower mandible, dark brown. Bill yellow. Legs cinereous.

Plate XLVII.

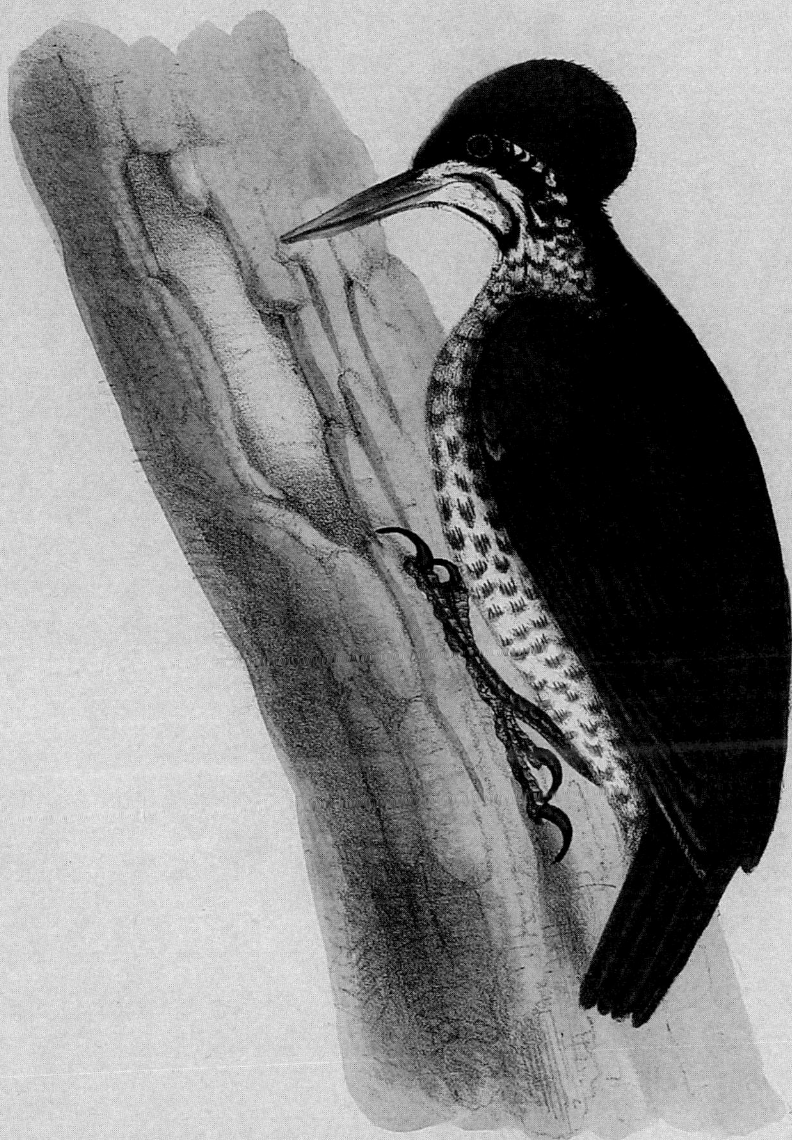

Miller lith. Reeve (London) imp.

PICUS ZEYLONUS

Plate XLVIII

Miller lith. Reeve (London) imp.

COLUMBA ELPHINSTONII

ORD. RASORES.

FAM. COLUMBIDÆ.

GEN. COLUMBA.

PLATE XLVIII.

COLUMBA ELPHINSTONII.

NEELGHERRY WOOD PIGEON.

Synon.—*Ptilinopus Elphinstonii*—Sykes—*C. pulchricollis*, Hodgs. ? ?

THIS handsome Pigeon I have only hitherto found in the dense woods on the summit of the Neelgherries, but as Sykes found it in the woods of the Western Ghats, I have no doubt that hereafter it will be ascertained to inhabit all the higher parts of that range of mountains. It is found single, or in small parties of four or five. It in general keeps to the woods, living on various fruit and berries, but occasionally it descends to the ground to procure various seeds and shells (Bulimi) which I have frequently found in its crop. I am unacquainted with its call and nidification, though it certainly breeds on the Neelgherries. Colonel Sykes, its original describer, makes it a *Ptilinopus*, but it is clearly (as Mr. Blyth ingeniously imagined from its mode of coloration alone, for he had not seen a specimen) a true *Columba* of the subdivision *Palumbus* or *Cushat*. Mr. Gray in his list of Hodgson's specimens presented to the British Museum, makes the *C. pulchricollis* of that gentleman a synonym of this Pigeon, which however I cannot assent to, on comparing the bird now before me with Mr. Blyth's copious description of *pulchricollis*. I add a description of *Elphinstonii*, which name I may mention was given in honor of the Governor of Bombay, the Hon. Mounstuart Elphinstone. Head, neck and plumage beneath ashy, the neck and breast glossed with green; a large nuchal mark black, the feathers tipped white; plumage above of a copper colour glossed slightly with purple and green. Quills and tail dusky black. Bill red, yellowish at the tip. Feet lake coloured. Irides yellow.

Length about 15 inches—wing $8\frac{1}{4}$—tail 6.

ORD. INSESSORES.

FAM. CRATEROPODINÆ.

GEN. XIPHORHAMPHUS.

PLATE XLIX.

XIPHORHAMPHUS SUPERCILIARIS.

SCIMITAR BILLED BABBLER.

Synon.—*Xiphirhynchus superciliaris*—Blyth, J. A. S., 1842, p. 175.

Mr. Blyth defines his genus *Xiphirhynchus*, afterwards changed to *Xiphorhamphus* on account of the first being preoccupied, as follows—Allied to *Pomatorhinus*, but the bill much longer and more slender, and very thinly compressed throughout its length, widening only at the extreme base, and describing a considerable incurvation. Plumage, wings, and tail as in *Pomatorhinus*, but the toes and claws rather more slender and elongated. I think that these characters hardly allow its separation from *Pomatorhinus*, being merely more *finely* expressed. This bird is "reported to be a pleasing Songster," but this is at variance with the known habits of most of the family. It inhabits Darjeeling.

Description.—Above uniform brown, the quills and tail dusky; beneath rufo-ferruginous; crown, occiput, and sides of the head, dark cinereous with a narrow superciliary white line extending to the occiput; throat whitish, streaked with grey; breast obscurely spotted with dusky; shoulders and tibial feathers dark grey; bill dusky; legs brown.

Length $8\frac{1}{2}$ inches—wing $2\frac{7}{8}$—tail $3\frac{3}{8}$—bill $1\frac{7}{8}$ in a straight line—tarsus 1—hind toe and claw 1.

The female differs in being slightly smaller, and in the colouring of the under parts being not so bright.

Plate XLIX.

R.E.B. lith.

XIPHORAMPHUS SUPERCILIARIS.

Plate. L.

R.E.B. lith. pre: lith: Lonn: imp.

INDICATOR XANTHONOTUS.

ORD. INSESSORES.

FAM. PICIDÆ.

GEN. INDICATOR.

PLATE L.

INDICATOR XANTHONOTUS—BLYTH.

YELLOW BACKED HONEY GUIDE.

I CONSIDER the discovery of this bird at Darjeeling as one of the most interesting among the numerous novelties Mr. Blyth has had occasion to describe during his sojourn in India.* The only recorded species belong to Africa, and the interest attached to their peculiar habits has been recorded by several travellers in that country, and has I believe been confirmed by recent writers. For the information of such as have not had an opportunity of becoming acquainted with these peculiarities, I may here mention, that the common African Honey Guide *(Indicator)* is said to direct the negroes by a peculiar cry or whistle to the tree where the bees have taken up their residence, advancing before them by longer or shorter flights according to the greater or less distance of the object of pursuit. As it approaches the tree, its flights become more limited, its whistle is repeated at shorter intervals, and at last, having brought its associates to the desired spot, it hovers over it for a moment as if to mark it out distinctly, and then quietly takes up a station at a little distance, waiting the result, and expecting its share of the booty, which it never fails to obtain. It would be interesting to know if our Indian Honey Guide has similar habits with its African congeners, and it is hoped that some resident at Darjeeling will endeavour to obtain some information on this subject.

I add a description of our bird.

Plumage generally of a dusky brown, tinged with green on the crown and back of the neck; forehead and throat pale yellow; rump fine golden yellow; beneath ashy with dark streaks; the lower tail-coverts blackish; tertiaries margined with white. Bill horny brown. Legs dusky.

Length 6 inches—wing 3⅜ths—tail 2¼—tarsus ½.

* Vide J. A. S., Bengal, 1842, page 166.

CLASSIFIED INDEX OF CONTENTS.